JOYCE'S DUBLIN:
A WALKING GUIDE TO 'ULYSSES'

To Robin, Megan and John

JOYCE'S DUBLIN:
A Walking Guide to 'Ulysses'

JACK McCARTHY

with maps by Bob Conrad

WOLFHOUND PRESS

© Jack McCarthy

Archive pictures from the Laurence Collection,
National Library, Dublin.

First published 1986 by Wolfhound Press,
68 Mountjoy Square, Dublin 1.

British Library Cataloguing in Publication Data

McCarthy, Jack
Joyce's Dublin: A walking guide to 'Ulysses'
1. Joyce, James, 1882-1941 — Homes and haunts —
Ireland — Dublin (Dublin)
I. Title
823'.912   PR6019.09Z/

ISBN 0-86327-110-3
ISBN 0-86327-115-4 PBK

Cover design by Jan de Fouw
Maps by Bob Conrad
Index map on pages 8-9 by E. Ryan
Typesetting and origination by Redsetter Ltd.
Printed by Brough, Cox and Dunn Ltd.

CONTENTS

INTRODUCTION

James Joyce once remarked that he was 'more interested in the street names of Dublin than in the riddle of the universe'. Dublin is a detailed presence in all of Joyce's works, but his classic novel *Ulysses*, published in 1922, put Dublin on the literary map and earned enduring fame for many Dublin places. *Ulysses* follows the wanderings of Stephen Dedalus and Leopold Bloom through Dublin on 16 June 1904 – known to Joyceans since the publication of *Ulysses* as 'Bloomsday'. On this day Joyce may have had his first date with Nora Barnacle, who was to become his lifelong companion (and eventually his wife). Joyce's father, hearing that his son had run off to the Continent with a woman named Barnacle, quipped, 'Well, she'll stick to him anyway'. The purpose of this book is to trace the routes that the main characters in *Ulysses* take through Dublin. Joyce makes it difficult for the reader to follow such paths. He even bragged about putting so many 'enigmas and puzzles' in *Ulysses* that it would keep the professors busy for centuries. This book is an attempt to clarify one aspect of Joyce's puzzle – which characters took what paths in Dublin. It can be used as a reference guide for those reading *Ulysses* and as a Dublin guide for those Joyce enthusiasts who want to follow in the footsteps of Stephen and Bloom. It is also intended for those who have never read *Ulysses* but are curious about the Dublin places Joyce mentions. No book of this length could cite all the Dublin places Joyce named in his work, but it does highlight much of the cityscape of *Ulysses*, with particular emphasis on what still exists today.

Like *Ulysses*, this book is divided into eighteen chapters. I have identified each chapter primarily by its geographic setting. In his text Joyce does not use chapter titles but each chapter has a reference to Homer's *Odyssey*: for example, Bloom's encounter with Gerty MacDowell recalls Odysseus' meeting with Nausicaa on the beach. Page and line references for quotations are given, based on the second Modern Library edition (Random House: New York, 1961). Many of the buildings shown on the maps do not necessarily depict actual structures but are meant to give an impression of the cityscape.

ACKNOWLEDGEMENTS

The author wishes to thank The Society of Authors as the literary representative of the Estate of James Joyce for permission to quote from *Ulysses*; the Ordnance Survey of Ireland, Phoenix Park, Dublin for permission to reproduce the maps of Dublin – Permit No. 4127; the National Library of Ireland, Dublin for permission to reproduce photographs from the Laurence Collection.

Special thanks are due to: Bob Conrad for drawing the maps, with additional help from Eilis Ryan, who also drew the index map; Conrad Jones for the photographs inset on the maps; Abigail Bok (U.S.) and Loretta Byrne for editing; and Susan Jabanolic and Patty Cherrington for word-processing and secretarial assistance.

With thanks also to A. Walton Litz (Princeton University), Clive Hart (University of Essex), David Norris (Trinity College, Dublin), Sean White (School of Irish Studies), and Don Gifford (Williams College) for advice and information. And finally thanks to Paul Gray, Lowell Miller, Brendan Halligan, Joe Marshall, Nigel Holmes for their generous assistance.

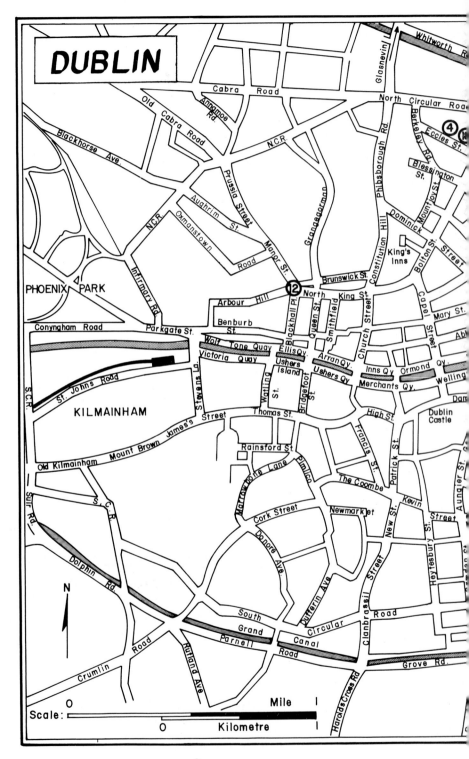

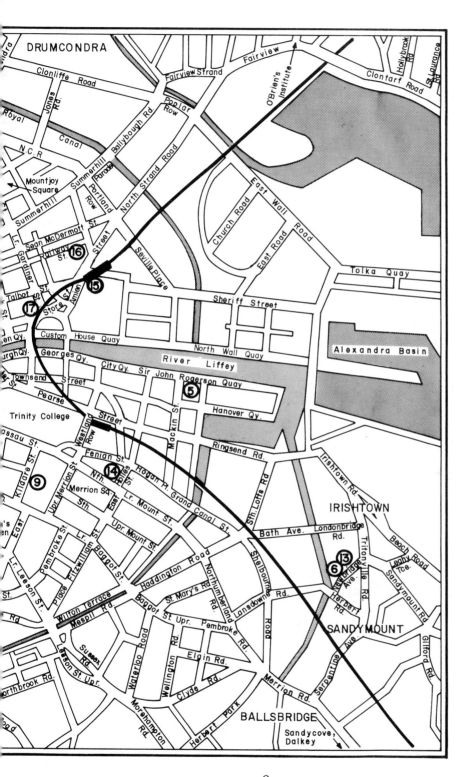

DRUMCONDRA

Clonliffe Road

Fairview Strand

Fairview

O'Brien's Institute

Clontarf Road

Hollybrook Rd.

Laurance Rd.

Jones Rd.

Poplar Row

Royal Canal

Ballybough Rd.

N.C.R

Summerhill Parade

Church Road

East Wall Road

East Road

Mountjoy Square

Portland Row

North Strand Road

Sevilla Place

Tolka Quay

Summerhill

Sean McDermott Street

Railway St. ⑯

Amien St.

Sheriff Street

Alexandra Basin

Lr. Gardiner St.

⑮

Talbot St.

⑰

Store St.

Custom House Quay

North Wall Quay

Georges Qy.

City Qy.

Sir John Rogerson Quay

River Liffey

⑤

Townsend Street

Hanover Qy.

Pearse Street

Ringsend Rd.

Trinity College

Westland Row

Nassau St.

Fenian St.

Irishtown Rd.

Kildare St.

⑨

Upr. Merrion St.

Merrion Sq.

Sth.

Lr. Mount St.

East

⑭

Holles St.

Rogan Pl.

Grand Canal St.

Sth. Lotts Rd.

IRISHTOWN

Beach Road

Upr. Mount St.

Leahy Tce.

East's

Pembroke St.

Fitzwilliam Place

Lr. Baggot St.

Haddington Road

Northumberland Rd.

Bath Ave. Londonbridge Rd.

Tritonville Rd.

⑥ ⑬

Newbridge Ave.

Sandymount Rd.

Lr. Leeson St.

Wilton Terrace

Mespil Rd.

St. Mary's Rd.

Lansdowne Rd.

Herbert Rd.

Gilford Rd.

Baggot St. Upr.

Pembroke Rd.

Shelbourne Rd.

SANDYMOUNT

Sussex Rd.

Waterloo Rd.

Elgin Rd.

Serpentine Ave.

Leeson St. Upr.

Wellington Rd.

Clyde Rd.

Merrion Rd.

Northbrook Rd.

Morehampton Rd.

Herbert Park

BALLSBRIDGE

Sandycove; Dalkey

Martello Tower, Sandycove
8.00 a.m. to 8.45 a.m.
(Telemachus)

Ulysses opens in the **Martello Tower** that stands on the shore of Dublin Bay in Sandycove Harbour, approximately seven miles southeast of the center of Dublin. The time is 8.00 a.m., Thursday, 16 June 1904. Martello towers took their name from the towers, 'mortella' in Italian, which the British first saw in Corsica and later erected (*circa* 1800) around the Irish and British coasts to repel an expected invasion by Napoleon. Sixteen Martello towers were built on the south side of Dublin, twelve on the north side. The one singled out in Joyce's novel is about forty feet high with walls eight feet thick; the original entrance was roughly ten feet off the ground. This strange, Bohemian residence was the 1904 Dublin equivalent to a hippy commune of the 1960s – a counterculture haven from the supposed conformity and blandness of traditional living arrangements. In this first episode of *Ulysses* Stephen Dedalus, a moody, brooding twenty-two-year-old poet and part-time teacher at a boys' school, and Buck Mulligan, a brash medical school student, are the tower's two tenants. An Englishman, Haines, is visiting them and wants to use Stephen as part of his study of Irish culture – which Stephen refuses to allow unless he is paid.

Joyce himself spent 9 through 14 September 1904 at this same tower with his sometime drinking partner, Oliver St John Gogarty (the model for Buck Mulligan) and another guest, Dermot Chevenix Trench (the model for Haines). During the night of 14 September, Trench had a nightmare and fired a revolver shot that almost hit Joyce, who left immediately, never to return. Trench's life ended five years later when he shot himself in the head, perhaps with the same gun.

At the start of *Ulysses*, Buck Mulligan is shaving in the open air at the top of the tower and mocking the ritual of the Catholic

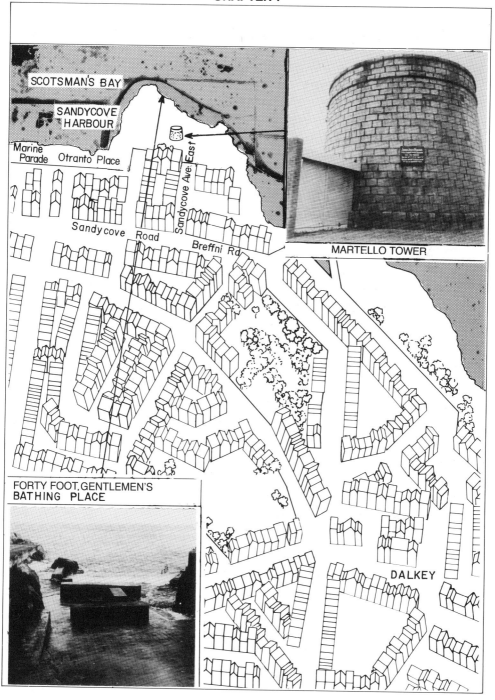

CHAPTER 1

SCOTSMAN'S BAY

SANDYCOVE HARBOUR

Marine Parade   Otranto Place

Sandycove   Road

Sandycove Ave. East

Breffni Rd.

MARTELLO TOWER

FORTY FOOT, GENTLEMEN'S BATHING PLACE

DALKEY

Mass. Stephen Dedalus joins him, and they discuss how long Haines plans to stay. Mulligan borrows Stephen's handkerchief, remarking that he has found a 'new art colour for our Irish poets: snotgreen' (5:1-2). To return the favor Mulligan offers to lend Stephen a pair of gray pinstripe pants, but Stephen declines the offer, saying that he won't wear gray trousers (because he is in mourning). Mulligan replies, 'He kills his mother but he can't wear grey trousers' (6:13-14) – a reference to Stephen's refusal of his mother's wish that he kneel and pray at her deathbed. The two go downstairs and have breakfast with Haines, who speaks in Gaelic to an Irish milkwoman making her rounds. Not understanding Gaelic, the milkwoman asks Haines if he is speaking French or comes from the west of Ireland. Mulligan explains, 'He's English . . . and he thinks we ought to speak Irish in Ireland' (14:34-35). Soon after the three men depart – Mulligan to take a morning swim in the **Forty-Foot: Gentlemen's Bathing Place** a few yards away, Haines to sit on a stone and smoke, and Stephen to walk to the Summerfield Lodge School about a mile away.

The illustration on page 11 shows the location of the Martello Tower at Sandycove and the Forty-Foot: Gentlemen's Bathing Place. Today this tower is preserved as the James Joyce Museum, though some alterations have been made. Men (and occasionally women) still swim at the nearby bathing spot.

How to get there: by DART (Dublin Area Rapid Transit) train from Amiens Street station; Tara Street station; Westland Row station. Or take a No. 8 bus from Eden Quay.

SEAPOINT. Co. DUBLIN. 1699. W. L.

13

Mr Deasy's School, Dalkey
9.40 A.M. TO 10.05 A.M.
(Nestor)

This chapter takes place entirely at the Summerfield Lodge School in Dalkey, a small town approximately one mile southeast of the Martello Tower at Sandycove. Stephen is teaching history and English to a bored class of boys and tries to entertain them by asking, 'What is a pier?' The answer: 'A disappointed bridge' (24:38, 25:4). After class he receives his month's pay from the school's proprietor, Mr Deasy, who also asks him to take a letter about foot-and-mouth disease in cattle to the editors of two Dublin newspapers. A bigoted Northern Ireland Protestant, Deasy claims that 'jew merchants' are destroying England. Stephen responds: 'A merchant . . . is one who buys cheap and sells dear, jew or gentile' (34:1-2). Their conversation ends as Deasy claims (quite incorrectly): 'Ireland . . . has the honour of being the only country which never persecuted the jews . . . . And do you know why? . . . Because she never let them in' (36:9-14). For a few months in 1904 Joyce taught part-time at the **Clifton School** in Dalkey (which became the model for Summerfield Lodge) where the founder and headmaster was an Ulsterman, Francis Irwin, the prototype of Mr Deasy.

The map shows the probable path that Stephen takes in walking from the Martello Tower in Sandycove to Mr Deasy's school on Dalkey Avenue in Dalkey. The building still exists but is no longer a school. Now a private residence, it is difficult to see from the road. Stephen leaves the Martello Tower at approximately 8.45 a.m. and walks to Summerfield Lodge, probably along Sandycove Avenue East, Breffni Road, Ulverton Road, and Dalkey Avenue. As a residential suburb of Dublin, Dalkey is more developed than it was in 1904, but still retains much of the atmosphere of an Irish village. (*How to get there:* see page 12)

CHAPTER 2

•••• Stephen's Probable Route
(not actually taken during this chapter)

Sandycove Ave. East

BULLOCK HARBOUR

Sandycove Road

Breffni Road

DEASY'S SUMMERFIELD LODGE SCHOOL

Ulverton Rd.

Castle St.

DALKEY

Dalkey Ave.

Sandymount Strand

11.00 A.M. TO 11.30 A.M.

(Proteus)

The scene of this chapter is **Sandymount Strand**, a beach just south of the Liffey River estuary near the Pigeonhouse, an electrical generating station. Stephen walks along the beach for approximately thirty minutes. This chapter is a record of Stephen's thoughts during which he recalls his school days, observes the happenings on the beach, and muses on various esoteric subjects. He speculates about books he was 'going to write with letters for titles. Have you read his F? O yes, but I prefer Q. Yes, but W is wonderful' (40:32-33). He makes jokes about Queen Victoria – 'the old hag with the yellow teeth' (43:13) – and 'Lawn Tennyson, gentleman poet' (50:32). The sight of the Pigeonhouse reminds him of an irreverent French joke about the Holy Family, which can be translated as: 'Who has put you in this wretched condition? It was the pigeon, Joseph' (41:14-15).

The illustration opposite shows the probable public transportation route that Stephen takes from Dalkey to Sandymount Strand and roughly where he walked on the beach. In all likelihood he catches the Bray-to-Dublin train at the Dalkey station, alighting at the Lansdowne Road station a few minutes later. Stephen has some extra time prior to a scheduled meeting with Buck Mulligan at 12.30 p.m. at a pub called The Ship (a meeting Stephen later decides to avoid). He thinks about paying a call to the house of his uncle, Richie Goulding, in Strasburg Terrace, Irishtown, but apparently never makes that visit. It is unclear whether Stephen walks or takes a tram to the newspaper office in the center of Dublin, where he is next seen, some time after noon. He does stop at the College Green Post Office to send a telegram to Buck Mulligan at The Ship, canceling the meeting. Stephen is heading towards the center of Dublin at approximately the same time that Leopold Bloom is traveling in the same direction with

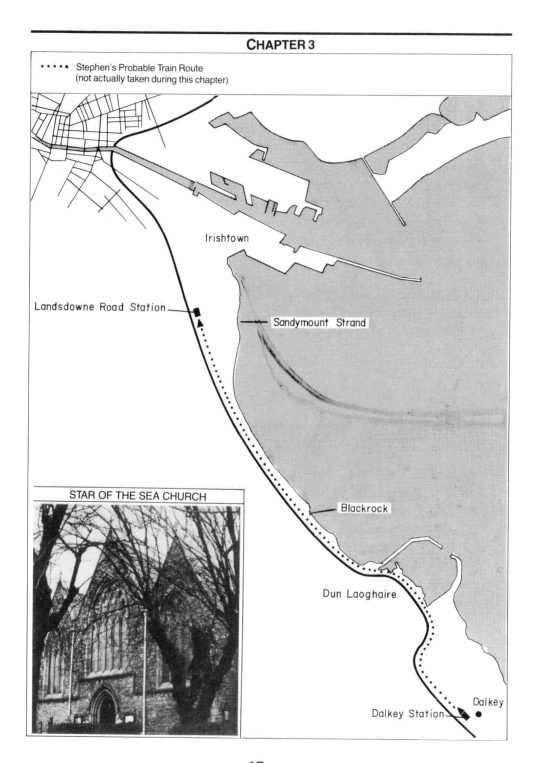

CHAPTER 3

• • • • • Stephen's Probable Train Route
(not actually taken during this chapter)

Irishtown

Landsdowne Road Station

Sandymount Strand

STAR OF THE SEA CHURCH

Blackrock

Dun Laoghaire

Dalkey

Dalkey Station

17

the funeral cortège (see Chapter Six). Today a Joycean can take a DART (Dublin Area Rapid Transit) train from the Dalkey station and, like Stephen, get off at the Lansdowne Road stop near Lansdowne Rugby Ground, Ireland's largest rugby stadium. Once outside the station walk down Newbridge Avenue, then turn right into Sandymount Road, left onto Marine Drive and then onto the Beach Road. The visitor today will find green parkland on some of the strand that Stephen walked since the north end of the beach has been reclaimed during the last thirty years. A grassy promenade area now covers the rocks at Leahy's Terrace, but the original sea wall is still visible there, separating the road from the grass instead of the sea.

How to get there: by DART (Dublin Area Rapid Transit) train from Amiens Street station; Tara Street station; Westland Row station to Lansdowne Road station or Sandymount station. Or take a No 3 bus from O'Connell Street.

19

No. 7 Eccles Street
8.00 a.m. to 8.45 a.m.
(Calypso)

In this chapter *Ulysses* jumps back in time to its starting point and we meet Leopold Bloom, a thirty-eight-year-old advertising salesman for a (now defunct) Dublin daily newspaper, the *Freeman's Journal*. Bloom is preparing breakfast for his thirty-three-year-old wife, Molly, an amateur opera singer about to perform in a Belfast concert arranged by her lover, Blazes Boylan. She is still half asleep, so he walks around the corner to buy a kidney from Dlugacz's butcher shop for his own breakfast, speculating on the way that a 'good puzzle would be cross Dublin without passing a pub' (58:25-26). While purchasing the pork kidney, Bloom thinks about following a female customer when she leaves the shop. But he discards the idea as she goes in the opposite direction from his house. When he returns, he cooks (actually burns) the kidney, brings his wife her breakfast in bed, feeds the cat, and reads a letter from his daughter Millie, who is working for a photographer in Mullingar, about fifty miles northwest of Dublin. Molly looks at her mail (which includes a letter from Boylan) and asks her husband to define a word for her: 'Metempsychosis? . . . Who's he when he's at home?' (64:18-19). The chapter ends with Bloom using an outdoor privy and hearing the bells of **St George's Church**.

The map on the facing page shows the Bloom house at **No. 7 Eccles Street** (now no longer in existence) and follows Bloom's course when he leaves to buy the kidney. He crosses over to the opposite side of Eccles Street, turns right at Larry O'Rourke's Pub at 72-73 Upper Dorset Street (now occupied by the Eccles Bar). He passes **St. Joseph's School** (now St Raphael's House) and buys the pork kidney at Dlugacz's butcher shop (one of the few entirely imaginary stores in *Ulysses*, though Dlugacz was a Triestine Jew that Joyce met after he left Dublin) on the northwest side of Dorset Street.

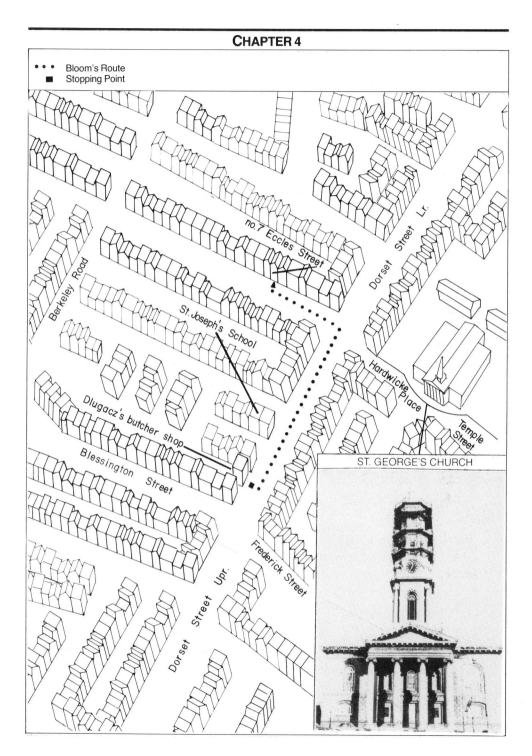

CHAPTER 4

Bloom's Route

■ Stopping Point

no.7 Eccles Street

Dorset Street Lr.

Berkeley Road

St. Joseph's School

Hardwicke Place

Dlugacz's butcher shop

Temple Street

Blessington Street

Dorset Street Upr.

Frederick Street

ST. GEORGE'S CHURCH

ST. GEORGES CHURCH, DUBLIN. 724 W. L.

22

South Dublin Streets
9.40 A.M. TO 10.05 A.M.
(Lotus Eaters)

After finishing breakfast, Bloom sets off at about 9.40 a.m. In this chapter he walks along the Liffey River and through a commercial district of Dublin. He makes three stops: first at a post office to pick up a letter, second at the **St Andrews** (which Joyce calls All Hallows) **Roman Catholic Church**, where he watches the priest celebrate Mass, and third at **Sweny's Chemist's Shop** (drug store).

As the map on the opposite page shows, Bloom's path from the Liffey to the **Westland Row Post Office** forms a question mark. It is clearly not the shortest path he could take. He may want to avoid going directly to the post office (in case he is being watched) because he is picking up a letter from a woman. Perhaps he is just wandering aimlessly through Dublin. In any case, he is first seen heading east along Sir John Rogerson's Quay, a dock area along the Liffey. Bloom turns right (south) on Lime Street, now a warehouse area with high stone walls, then takes the first right, onto Hanover Street (which becomes Townsend Street). His walk along Lime and Hanover Streets is only briefly mentioned in the novel. After taking a left onto Lombard Street East, he notices the Salvation Army Hall called Bethel (71:13) and the offices of Nichols the undertaker – which is still at No. 26-31. He crosses Great Brunswick Street (now known as Pearse Street) and heads down Westland Row past the Grosvenor Hotel, which was demolished in the early 1980s, pausing in front of the Belfast and Oriental Tea Company storefront at No. 6 Westland Row under the train tracks. Bloom then crosses the street to pick up a letter from Martha Clifford (whom he has never met but with whom he is secretly corresponding) at the Westland Row Post Office. This post office no longer exists, but the building that housed it remains part of the Westland Row

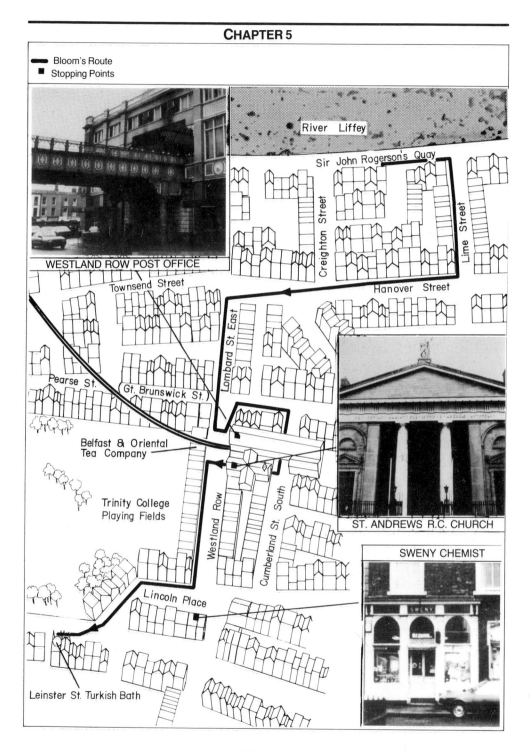

CHAPTER 5

Bloom's Route
Stopping Points

River Liffey

Sir John Rogerson's Quay

Creighton Street

Lime Street

Hanover Street

WESTLAND ROW POST OFFICE

Townsend Street

Lombard St. East

Pearse St.

Gt. Brunswick St.

Belfast & Oriental Tea Company

Trinity College Playing Fields

Westland Row

Cumberland St. South

ST. ANDREWS R.C. CHURCH

SWENY CHEMIST

Lincoln Place

Leinster St. Turkish Bath

station (Pearse station), the site of Ireland's first train run in 1834.

The second part of Bloom's route is from the post office to St Andrews (All Hallows). The map shows that once more Bloom goes far out of his way, his path again tracing the shape of a question mark. Upon leaving the post office, he turns to the right and has a brief conversation with an acquaintance named M'Coy, but succeeds in getting 'rid of him quickly' (73:13). Bloom retraces his steps back down Westland Row, turns right on Brunswick Street, and takes another right onto Cumberland Street, where he pauses. The secluded underpass beneath the train tracks provides a perfect spot to read Martha's letter in private. He then continues for a few steps in the same direction and turns right through the back entrance to All Hallows, where he watches Mass from the Communion to the end of the service. He speculates idly about the Host: 'Rum idea: eating bits of a corpse why the cannibals cotton to it' (80:37-38). St Andrew's Church was one of the first Catholic churches built in Ireland after Catholic Emancipation of 1829 (which allowed Catholics to enter the British Parliament), a movement led by Daniel O'Connell. O'Connell was a parishioner of St Andrews and instrumental in selecting the site for the church.

Bloom takes a more direct path to his third stop in the chapter – **Sweny's Chemist's Shop**. Leaving All Hallows by the main entrance, he makes a left turn to head south along Westland Row. At the intersection of Westland Row and Lincoln Place, he enters Sweny's, where he orders some skin lotion for Molly and buys lemon soap for fourpence. Though prominently displaying the new ownership of M. F. Quinn on the storefront, the shop in Lincoln Place still keeps the name Sweny. The original sign was rediscovered in 1982 when the shop front was being redecorated. Now it stands as a conspicuous tribute to the Joyce industry. 'Chemists rarely move,' Bloom correctly predicted (84:4). Sweny's still stocks lemon soap (though not the brand it carried in 1904). The chapter ends with Bloom taking a bath at the **Turkish and Warm Baths**, in Leinster St., demolished in the 1960s.

How to get there: see index map. Within walking distance of O'Connell Street.

26

FUNERAL PROCESSION
ACROSS DUBLIN

11.00 A.M. TO ABOUT 11.45 A.M.

(Hades)

In this episode Bloom travels with the funeral procession accompanying the body of Paddy Dignam (who died from a stroke) from the Dignam house in Sandymount, a suburb on the coast just southeast of Dublin, across Dublin to the Prospect Cemetery in Glasnevin (commonly known as **Glasnevin Cemetery**), in the northwest part of town, where Irish patriots such as Daniel O'Connell and Charles Stewart Parnell are buried. This chapter contains the longest single journey of main characters in *Ulysses*, a trek of about four miles. Bloom rides in a carriage with Stephen's father Simon Dedalus and two others. At Glasnevin Cemetery Bloom attends the service in the chapel and follows the mourners to the grave side. He then strikes off for the newspaper office in the center of Dublin. While many chapters of *Ulysses* show characters walking through Dublin, this episode constitutes one of the few instances in which the trip is made on wheels. Perhaps only hardy Joyceans should try to walk it today.

The map on the facing page shows the route of the funeral procession. To get to Sandymount, Bloom apparently takes the Sandymount (Haddington Road) tram line, boarding near the Turkish and Warm Baths and disembarking near Dignam's house. The funeral cortège starts at **No. 9 Newbridge Avenue** (87:29) in Sandymount and takes an initial route roughly parallel to the shore of Dublin Bay. One of the passengers, Martin Cunningham, outlines the first part of the journey – 'Irishtown . . . Ringsend. Brunswick street' (87:40-41). The carriage goes north on Tritonville Road into Irishtown Road and then on Thomas Street in Irishtown, an old fishing village. Thomas Street no longer exists; it is now part of Irishtown Road. The carriage

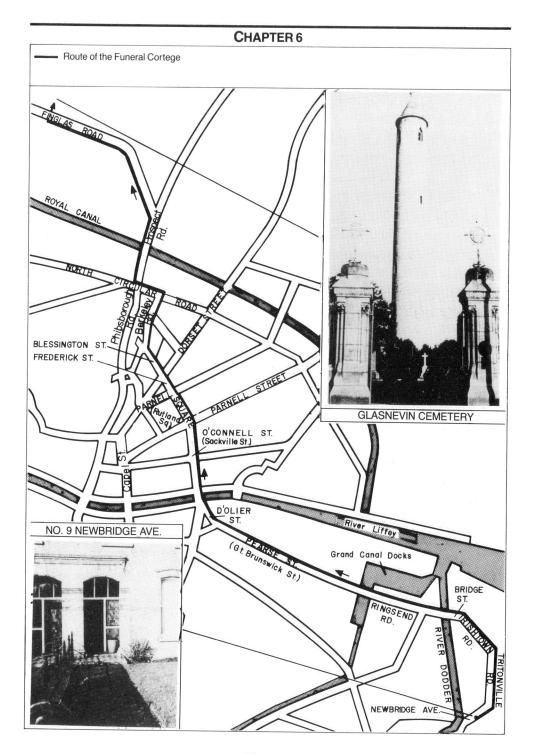

CHAPTER 6

Route of the Funeral Cortege

FINGLAS ROAD

ROYAL CANAL

NORTH CIRCULAR ROAD

Prospect Rd.

Phibsborough Rd.

Berkeley Rd.

DORSET STREET

BLESSINGTON ST.
FREDERICK ST.

PARNELL SQUARE
(Rutland Sq.)

PARNELL STREET

Capel St.

O'CONNELL ST.
(Sackville St.)

D'OLIER ST.

River Liffey

PEARSE ST.
(Gt. Brunswick St.)

Grand Canal Docks

RINGSEND RD.

BRIDGE ST.

IRISHTOWN RD.

RIVER DODDER

TRITONVILLE RD.

NEWBRIDGE AVE.

GLASNEVIN CEMETERY

NO. 9 NEWBRIDGE AVE.

turns west (left) onto Bridge Street which becomes first Ringsend Road and then Great Brunswick Street (now Pearse Street) – all heading towards the center of Dublin. After going down the short D'Olier Street onto Sackville Street (now O'Connell Street) across the Liffey River, the procession then goes by way of Parnell Square, Blessington Street, Berkeley Street, North Circular Road, Phibsborough Road, Prospect Road, and Finglas Road, arriving at **Glasnevin Cemetery**.

The passengers in the carriage see a number of Dublin places and people. Bloom sees Stephen – for the first time that day – as they pass Watery Lane in Irishtown: 'clad in mourning, a wide hat' (88:6). Stephen's mother (and also Joyce's mother) had died in Dublin in August 1903, and both were buried in Glasnevin. The entourage passes the Grand Canal (which was once a route of great importance, linking Dublin with the west of Ireland) and the 'gasworks', a foul-smelling plant in which coal was turned into liquefied gas. Bloom remarks, trying to relieve the gloom, 'Whooping cough they say it cures' (90:15). After the party passes the Antient Concert Rooms (91:40), now housing the Academy theater and various shops at 42 Great Brunswick Street – where Joyce sang with the famous Irish tenor John MacCormack on 27 August, 1904– Bloom boasts that his wife Molly will soon do a concert in Belfast with 'all topnobbers. J. C. Doyle and John MacCormack, . . . the best in fact' (93:7-8). The carriage goes down D'Olier Street (where Blazes Boylan has his offices, probably at number 15) and passes the statue of William Smith O'Brien, a leader of the 1848 rising (which has since been moved from the junction of D'Olier and Westmoreland Streets north to O'Connell Street), and next 'the hugecloaked Liberator's form' (93:39), the twelve-foot, bronze figure of Daniel O'Connell, nineteenth-century Irish patriot, famous for addressing tens of thousands at outdoor 'monster' rallies, here wrapped in his well-known cloak atop a twenty-eight foot limestone base and pedestal. Bloom muses that the commercial tenants occupying Sackville Street are a boring lot: 'Dead side of the street this. Dull business by day, land agents, temperance hotel, Falconer's railway guide, civil service college, Gill's, catholic club, the

ROTUNDA HOSPITAL, DUBLIN. 3473 W.L.

31

industrious blind . . . . Under the patronage of the late Father Mathew. Foundation stone for Parnell.' (95:35-40). Most of the buildings and businesses he mentions are no longer there, much of Sackville Street having been destroyed in the 1916 Rising and the 1922 Civil War. For example, the site of the Edinburgh Temperance Hotel at 56 Sackville Street Upper was a gunpowder office by 1916; it was occupied by rebel forces during the rising and was hit by bullets and shells. Maguire's Civil Service College (once 52 Sackville Street Upper) has been demolished, and the Richmond National Institution for the Instruction of the Industrious Blind (No. 41) is now part of the Royal Dublin Hotel. The Catholic Commercial Club at 42 Sackville Street Upper, once the elite preserve of Dublin's Catholic business and political leaders, no longer functions but the building, O'Connell Street's last Georgian structure, is still standing.

The procession passes the Rotunda (95:42), a series of buildings at the intersection of Sackville Street Upper and Cavendish Road (now Parnell Street), originally opened in 1757 as a 'lying-in hospital' or maternity hospital and expanded to include assembly halls, which now house the Gate Theatre and a cinema. Then the carriage turns northwest by Frederick Street from Rutland Square (now Parnell Square) to Blessington Street and Berkeley Street (97:18), where a street-organ plays 'Has Anybody Here Seen Kelly' (a song that was not in fact written until after 1904). Any Joycean today trying to drive the funeral cortège route will find that Frederick and Blessington Streets are now one-way streets going the wrong way for their purpose. Bloom and the others pass the Mater Misericordiae (97:22) – the largest hospital in Dublin at the time – at the intersection of Berkeley Road (the continuation of Berkeley Street) and Eccles Street where Bloom lives. The procession turns left (west) onto the North Circular Road, then right at Dunphy's Corner onto Phibsborough Road. Dunphy's Corner was named for a well-known pub operated by Thomas Dunphy until roughly 1918 at 160-161 Phibsborough Road. Long-time residents of that area still recall when Dunphy's pub was a famous stop after a burial at Glasnevin Cemetery. Today J. R. Murphy and Sons, vintners, run a pub recently renamed Sir Arthur Conan Doyle at this location. The corner is now known as Doyle's corner, not for the author of the Sherlock Holmes stories, but after the Doyle family who ran this pub for a number of generations up to the 1960s.

The entourage crosses the **Royal Canal** (99:8) – which Joyce describes in terms suggestive of the mythical river Styx – over the **Cross Guns Bridge** (a pub at the bridge is still called the Cross Guns). Just to the north of the bridge they pass 'Brian Boroimhe house' (99:25), a pub at No. 1 Prospect Terrace on the corner of Prospect Road named for Brian Boru, king of Ireland around the year 1000 who defeated the Danes at Clontarf (about a mile west of the pub) in 1014, but was killed afterwards by his own allies. This pub exists today; the Hedigan family has owned the business since November 1904 and the building has been there since about 1850. Finally, the carriage turns left onto Finglas Road, the southern boundary of **Glasnevin Cemetery**. Thos. H. Dennany's (99:37) display of cemetery markers was just off Finglas Road on Prospect Avenue but is no longer there (on the site today is a flower shop) but near the site is a tombstone shop. The house where 'Childs was murdered' (100:2) was located at 5 Bengal Terrace. Samuel Childs was tried (and acquitted) for the murder of his seventy-six-year-old brother at that house near Glasnevin Cemetery. Today's visitor can still see the 'dark poplars' and 'high railings of Prospects' (100:22-23), where the carriage stops and the mourners walk to the grave.

How to get there: by DART train from Amiens Street station; Tara Street station; Westland Row station to Lansdowne Road station. Or take a No. 3 bus from O'Connell Street.

THE FREEMAN'S JOURNAL

12.00 NOON TO 1.00 P.M.

(Aeolus)

This chapter takes place for the most part at the former offices of the *Freeman's Journal* and *Evening Telegraph* at 4-8 **Prince's Street North**, just off O'Connell Street. This is another of the chapters in which Stephen and Bloom cross paths but do not meet. In this repeated overlapping Joyce is not just taking literary license: in 1904 the population of Dublin was around 300,000 (today it is over 1 million) and Dubliners knew each other, knew about each other, and often met by chance on the streets and in shops and offices. At about noon Bloom sees the editor of the *Freeman's Journal* to discuss the renewal of an advertisement for Alexander Keyes, wine merchant (the editor eventually tells Bloom that Keyes 'can kiss my royal Irish arse' (147:11). At the same time Stephen Dedalus is presenting a copy of his letter from Mr Deasy on foot-and-mouth disease to the paper. Stephen's father, Simon Dedalus, and another Dubliner stop in at the offices of the *Freeman's Journal* and then leave to get a drink. Bloom departs for the National Library to look for a copy of a country newspaper, *The Kilkenny People*, from which he can get the exact form of the Keyes advertisement. As the chapter concludes, Stephen casts the deciding vote for a drink at **Mooney's Pub** across O'Connell Street at No. 1 Lower Abbey Street, where he buys the rounds.

The illustration opposite shows the former location of the newspaper offices at 4-8 **Prince's Street North** (now occupied by British Home Stores) near the Dublin General Post Office and the routes taken by various characters in this chapter. Bloom enters the newspaper building via the printing department, leaves to speak to his client, Mr Keyes (who is said to be at **Dillon's Auction Rooms** at 25 Bachelor's Walk), and returns to the newspaper office. Also shown are the paths taken to pubs – by Simon Dedalus and his friend to the **Oval Pub** at 78 Middle

CHAPTER 7

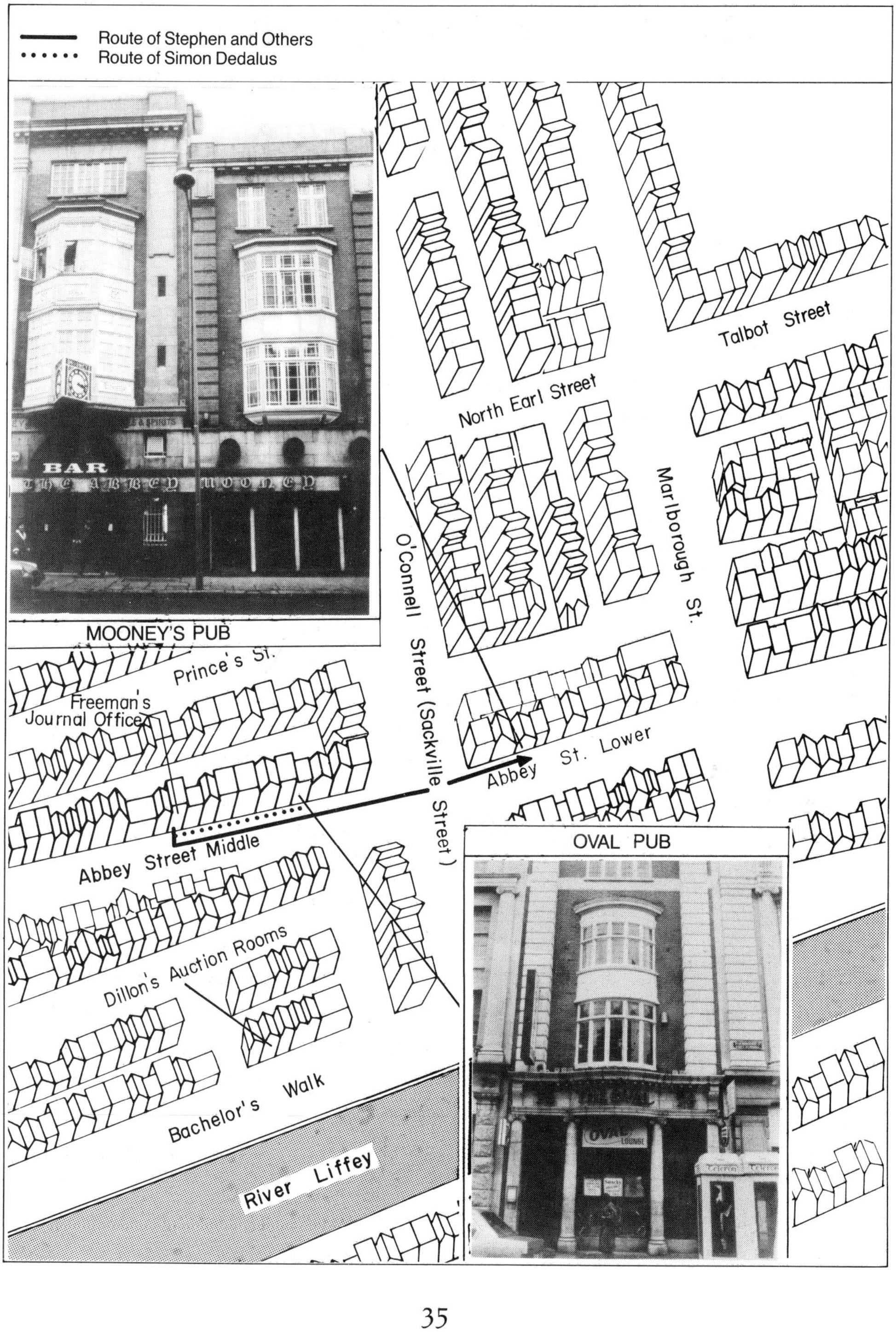
Route of Stephen and Others
Route of Simon Dedalus
MOONEY'S PUB
OVAL PUB
BAR
Talbot Street
North Earl Street
Marlborough St.
O'Connell Street (Sackville Street)
Prince's St.
Freeman's Journal Office
Abbey St. Lower
Abbey Street Middle
Dillon's Auction Rooms
Bachelor's Walk
River Liffey
OVAL

Abbey Street and by Stephen Dedalus and others from the Abbey Street exit of the newspaper building across O'Connell Street to Mooney's Pub. The Oval still serves Guinness stout at the same site, looking from the exterior much as it did in 1904. Mooney's Pub also remains in its 1904 location, but the exterior has been extensively remodeled. Dillon's Auction Rooms no longer occupy 25 Bachelor's Walk; in 1985 the Pierrot Club and other retail establishments rented the space.

How to get there: see location on index map. Just off O'Connell Street.

O'CONNELL STATUE. DUBLIN. 715. W.L.

Lunch At Davy Byrne's

1.00 P.M. TO 2.00 P.M.

(Lestrygonians)

This chapter covers Bloom's walk from the offices of the *Freeman's Journal* to the **National Museum**. He travels south across the Liffey River (stopping to buy two Banbury cakes to feed the birds) and has lunch at **Davy Byrne's Pub**, which is still serving food and drink today at 21 Duke Street. He then goes east to the National Library. Much of the chapter is about Bloom's observations and thoughts on a variety of subjects, from exporting Guinness stout to the secret 'cells' of the Irish Republican Brotherhood.

Bloom's route is shown on page 39, starting at O'Connell Street (then called Sackville Street). He walks southwards, passing **Lemon and Company, Ltd.**, a candy shop and small factory that was then located at No. 49, and reads or recalls their advertisement 'Lozenge and comfit manufacturer to His Majesty the King', picturing his highness 'on his throne, sucking red jujubes white' (151:3-5). Today a visitor can see over the Old Bridge Restaurant the name 'The Confectioners Hall' remaining from the days of Lemon's sweet shop. Bloom also looks down Bachelor's Walk to the right, to see **Butler's Monument House** (a musical instrument warehouse that was at No. 34) and Dillon's Auction Rooms (Joseph Dillon, auctioneer and valuer, 25 Bachelor's Walk), where he notices Stephen's destitute sister 'selling off some old furniture' (151:34). While crossing over the Liffey River on O'Connell Bridge (officially changed from Carlisle Bridge to O'Connell Bridge in 1882), he sees a barge with Guinness stout being exported to England and imagines rats on the ship getting 'dead drunk on the porter' (152:17-18). Now on the south side of the Liffey, Bloom passes the **Ballast Office** at 19-21 Westmoreland Street, which housed the offices of the Dublin Port and Docks Board in 1904. The Ballast Office has been remodeled with the clock on the Liffey side instead of the other side of the building as it was in 1904. He then meets Mrs Breen, an old acquaintance, and talks with her about her slightly demented husband (who dreamed the ace of spades was walking up the stairs). Continuing, Bloom walks by **The Irish Times** office at 31 Westmoreland Street (now occupied by the Educational Building Society), recalling the advertisement he placed that brought him into contact with Martha Clifford: 'Wanted smart lady typist to aid gentleman in literary work'. (160:11-12). He walks on 'past Bolton's Westmoreland House' (161:20, William Bolton and Company, grocers, tea, wine, and spirit merchants, 35-36 Westmoreland Street, the site now owned by the Allied Irish Banks). Near the 'Irish house of parliament' (162:13); the Bank of Ireland building was the Irish Parliament building until Great Britain dissolved the Irish Parliament by the Act of Union effective in 1800, Bloom speculates about what the pigeons above might be saying: 'Who will we do it on? I pick the fellow in the black. Here goes. Here's good luck' (162:14-16). Bloom 'crossed under Tommy Moore's roguish finger' (162:29) – a statue, still standing, of the nineteenth-century Irish poet Thomas Moore, who left Ireland to become a favorite in British aristocratic circles. Bloom thinks: 'They did right to put him up over a urinal: meeting of the waters' (162:29-30) – a common Dublin joke and a reference to his poem 'The Meeting of the Waters' in *Irish Melodies*. Seeing **Trinity College** (which until the 1970s a Catholic could suffer excommunication for attending), Bloom recalls the young students who protested against British Prime Minister Joseph Chamberlain receiving an honorary degree in 1899 and predicts: 'Few years' time half of them magistrates and civil servants' (163:14-15). He then passes 'Trinity's surly front' (164:16), the massive stone façade of the university. Next on Bloom's route are the Trinity College Provost's House (which still stands) and 'Walter Sexton's window' (165:2) across the street from the provost's house (Walter Sexton, goldsmith, jeweler, silversmith, and watchmaker, at 118 Grafton Street, a site now occupied by a Thomas Cook Travel Agency). In front of the windows of **Yeates and Sons** (which stood at the corner of

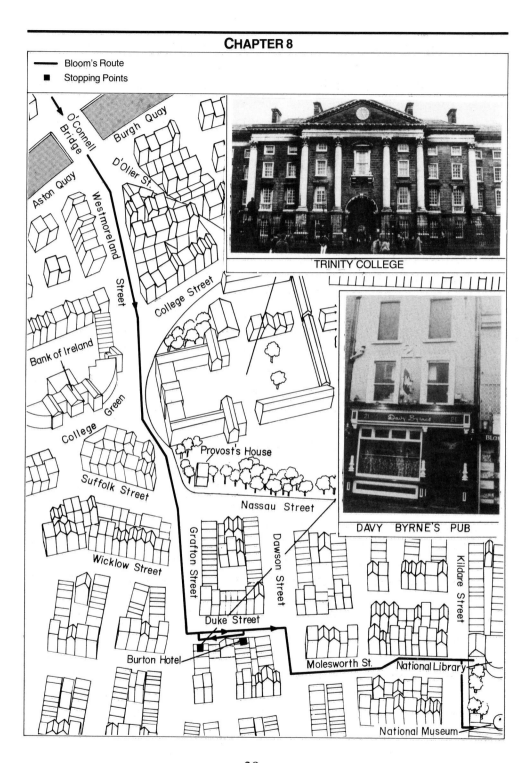

CHAPTER 8

Bloom's Route
Stopping Points

O'Connell Bridge
Burgh Quay
D'Olier St.
Aston Quay
Westmoreland Street
College Street
Bank of Ireland
College Green
Suffolk Street
Wicklow Street
Provost's House
Nassau Street
Grafton Street
Dawson Street
Duke Street
Burton Hotel
Molesworth St.
National Library
Kildare Street
National Museum

TRINITY COLLEGE

DAVY BYRNE'S PUB

Grafton and Nassau Streets until the 1970s) Bloom pauses 'pricing the field glasses' (166:18) and mentally notes how Germany has increased such exports: 'Germans making their way everywhere' (166:21-22). After passing La Maison Claire (a court milliner and dressmaker no longer at 4 Grafton Street) and Adam Court, a tiny passageway still off Grafton Street, Bloom's surroundings 'gay with housed awnings lured his senses' (168:10). Then, as today, Grafton Street was the fashionable shopping street of Dublin. He passes, 'dallying, the windows of Brown Thomas, silk mercers' (168:17-18). Brown Thomas claimed in 1904 that it had the best Irish lace and linen; its product line has expanded considerably, for today it is one of Dublin's finest department stores.

Bloom's next wandering in this chapter takes him to Duke Street (off Grafton Street) in search of something to eat. He turns at Combridge's Corner (Combridge and Co, picture depot, print sellers, picture-frame makers, artists, and colorman at 20 Grafton Street on the intersection of Duke Street – now part of Brown Thomas, while Combridge's has moved to Suffolk Street). He first stops in the Burton, formally known as the Burton Hotel and Billiard Rooms, at 18 Duke Street, where he is disgusted by what he sees: 'Stink gripped his trembling breath: pungent meatjuice, slop of greens. See the animals feed' (169:9-10). Leaving the Burton, Bloom backtracks three shopfronts to **Davy Byrne's** at 21 Duke Street, which for many years bore on its sign Bloom's description of it: 'Moral pub' (171:20). Bloom recalls Davy Byrne: 'He doesn't chat. Stands a drink now and then. But in leapyear once in four' (171:20-21). For lunch Bloom has a glass of burgundy and a Gorgonzola cheese sandwich with mustard while chatting with Nosey Flynn, whose mouth is so big he 'could whistle in his own ear' (172:21). After lunch Bloom turns right towards Dawson Street, passing Duke Lane and 'William Miller, plumber' at 17 Duke Street (179:40-41). Walking further he looks across the street at John Long's, a pub at 52 Dawson Street on the corner of Duke Street – now a delicatessen called Graham O'Sullivan – then turns right (south) onto Dawson Street near 'Gray's confectioner's window' (180:24; 13 Duke Street, a

41

42

site now occupied by a newsagent. He passes the Rev. Thomas Connellan's Bookstore at 51B Dawson Street, an establishment specializing in protestant evangelical tracts (now that address houses the Tea Time Express, a cake shop, and a visitor today can still see the display window once used for books). The sight of a bakery and a religious bookstore reminds Bloom of the connection between food and religion: 'They say they used to give pauper children soup to change to protestants in the time of the potato blight' (180:27-28). Bloom helps a blind youth across Dawson Street and passes Drago's (Adolphe Drago, perfumer and hairdresser, at 17 Dawson Street), the Stewart Institution for Imbecile Children at 40 Molesworth Street, and Doran's Pub at 10 Molesworth Street – all of these buildings have been demolished and the area extensively redeveloped. The map also shows how Bloom changes direction when, continuing into Kildare Street, he turns left to enter the National Library, but then catches sight of Blazes Boylan, who is going to rendezvous that afternoon with Bloom's wife, Molly. To avoid meeting Boylan, Bloom veers away from the National Library and instead turns right and heads for the **National Museum**. The chapter ends with Bloom looking at the statues known as the Goddesses.

How to get there: see location on index map. Start from O'Connell Street.

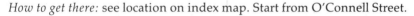

The National Library
2.00 P.M. TO 2.45 P.M.
(*Scylla and Charybdis*)

After spending the preceding hour buying drinks at Mooney's Pub for his acquaintances from the newspaper office, Stephen Dedalus is now seen at the **National\Library**, Kildare Street, where he talks about his interpretation of *Hamlet* with some very distinguished Dubliners: AE (George Russell) the writer, W. K. Magee, who used the nom-de-plume 'John Eglinton', the Quaker librarian, Thomas Lyster and the assistant librarian R. I. Best, an accomplished Celtic scholar who was an acquaintance of Joyce, Synge and many other important figures in the Irish literary revival. Mulligan arrives in the middle of Stephen's discourse. Bloom also enters the library, once again crossing paths with Stephen but not meeting. While the discussion about *Hamlet* is going on, Bloom copies the advertisement he needs from the *Kilkenny People*. Stephen and Mulligan leave the library about 3.00 p.m., passing Bloom.

How to get there: see location on index map. 15 minutes walk from O'Connell Street. Or take Nos. 10/11/14/ bus from O'Connell Street.

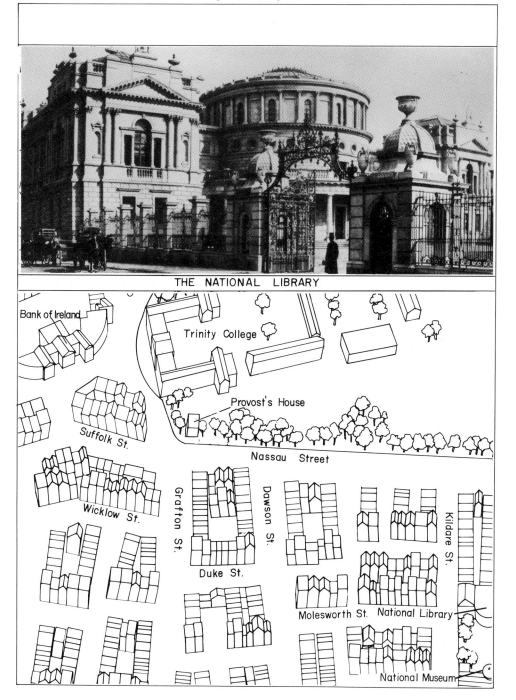

CHAPTER 9

THE NATIONAL LIBRARY

Bank of Ireland

Trinity College

Provost's House

Suffolk St.

Nassau Street

Grafton St.

Dawson St.

Wicklow St.

Kildare St.

Duke St.

Molesworth St.   National Library

National Museum

City Odyssey

2.55 P.M. TO 4.00 P.M.

(Wandering Rocks)

This chapter comprises nineteen short scenes involving various Dubliners in different parts of the city. This is an 'odyssey within an odyssey'. In a few of the scenes we see Bloom and Stephen, who have both left the library and are looking at books on open stalls near the Liffey. The longest scenes in this episode are the first and last. The first section describes a walk taken by Father John Conmee, former rector of Stephen's school, Clongowes Wood, and the last section, the progress of the viceregal cavalcade from Phoenix Park in northwest Dublin to a bazaar at the Royal Dublin Society in Ballsbridge in the southeast part of the city.

The maps on pages 50-51 detail the routes of both Father Conmee and the viceregal cavalcade, representing the spiritual and temporal powers that held sway in Dublin in 1904 – the Roman Catholic Church and the British government. It also shows the routes of the minor characters, each marked by the appropriate section number from the 'Wandering Rocks' episode. The nineteen episodes are summarized below.

I: This is Father Conmee's walk from the Presbytery of the **Church of St. Francis Xavier** on Upper Gardiner Street to the O'Brien Institute. He passes through Mountjoy Square, once a prosperous area of Georgian townhouses, turns left on Great Charles Street and then right onto the North Circular Road – which was the northern boundary of Dublin in 1904 – passing Richmond Street, a short, dead-end road off the North Circular Road, where he encounters a group of students from the Christian Brothers' School on the corner. North Circular Road becomes Portland Row, where Conmee passes St Joseph's Roman Catholic Church and St Joseph's Asylum for Aged and Virtuous Females

47

– now just called St Joseph's Home for Aged Females – at 4-8 Portland Row. He next passes Aldborough House, one of the last Palladian mansions to be built in Ireland, commissioned in the late eighteenth century by Lord Aldborough for his wife (who refused to live there). The Irish Post Office bought and occupied the building in 1904, and continues to do so. Conmee turns left onto North Strand Road and is 'saluted' by Mr William Gallagher, who stands in the doorway of his grocery shop at No 4 North Strand Road. Conmee also passes on North Strand Road Grogan's tobacconist's at No 16, Daniel Bergin's Pub at No 17, Youkstetter's pork-butcher shop at No 21, and on the opposite side of the Street **H. J. O'Neill's** funeral establishment at No 164 (the firm that handled the Dignam burial) – all of which have since been demolished for public housing. He crosses the Royal Canal at Newcomen Bridge, where he boards a tram that crosses the Tolka River at Annesley Bridge. The part of Dublin Bay to Father Conmee's right, which was mud flats in 1904, has been partially reclaimed to make Fairview Park. Conmee completes his journey via Fairview Road and Malahide Road to the O'Brien Institute for Destitute Children (whose grounds contain the beautifully restored Georgian Marino Casino, a garden pavilion built by the great English architect, William Chambers, for Lord Charlemont) where he intends to urge the provision of a place for the orphaned son of Paddy Dignam.

II: Corny Kelleher, the undertaker, is seen spitting while he works at **H. J. O'Neill's** undertaker's establishment at 164 North Strand Road.

III: The map shows the path of a one-legged sailor along Dorset Street and Eccles Street, passing MacConnell's corner, named for Andrew MacConnell, pharmaceutical chemist at 112 Dorset Street Lower (the site is now a grocery store called The Corner Shop). He passes the Bloom residence at **No 7 Eccles Street**, where Molly tosses him a coin.

IV: This scene takes place at **No 7 St Peter's Terrace, Cabra**, the home of the Joyce family in June 1904. Stephen's sisters, Katey and Boody, have walked home from school by way of Eccles Street, Berkeley Road, North Circular Road, and Cabra Road. They are seen washing shirts and complaining about how little money the family has. Boody mentions their sister Dilly, who has gone to find their 'father who art not in heaven' (227:3).

V: Molly's lover, Blazes Boylan, buys port, potted meat, and fruits for her from **Thornton's**, a fruit shop and florist at No 63 Grafton Street, now part of Dunne's Stores Ltd.

VI: Carrying his ashplant, Stephen meets his music teacher, Almidano Artifoni, at the **Trinity College** front gates opposite the Bank of Ireland.

VII: The scene depicted is Blazes Boylan's office in central Dublin, probably **The Advertising Co.** at No 15 D'Olier Street (the premises now shared by one of *The Irish Times* offices and a photography studio), where the secretary is waiting for the day to end.

VIII: Ned Lambert shows a clergyman, Rev. Hugh C. Love, the vaulted arches of the chapter house (meeting room) of **St Mary's Abbey**, then stands chatting with J. J. O'Molloy. In 1904 Alexander and Co., seed merchants, had offices at 2-5 Mary's Abbey, and their warehouse included the old chapter house. Today a visitor can still see the chapter house by obtaining a key from either the Junk Shop or Klein's Carpet Warehouse.

IX: The chart shows the path of two minor characters, Lenehan and M'Coy, as they walk from Crampton Court to Grattan Bridge, commonly known as Capel Street Bridge, on Wellington Quay. This is a very roundabout route to their destination, the **Ormond Hotel**; apparently Lenehan has some extra time. The two talk, and Lenehan tells stories about brushing up against Molly Bloom. Leaving Crampton Court just south of Grattan Bridge, the two turn left onto Dame Street passing 'Dan Lowry's

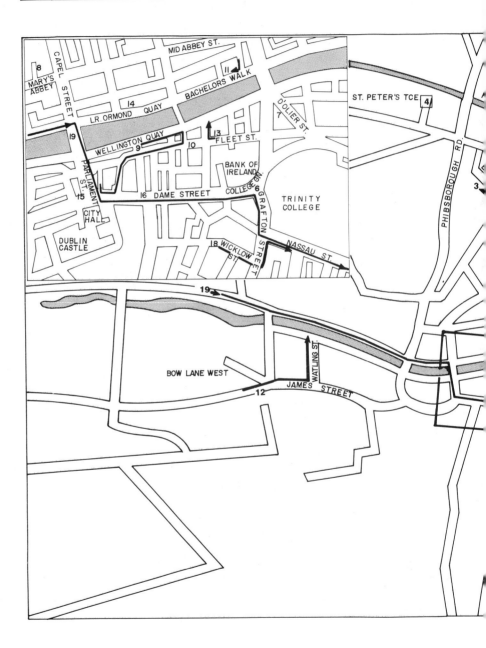

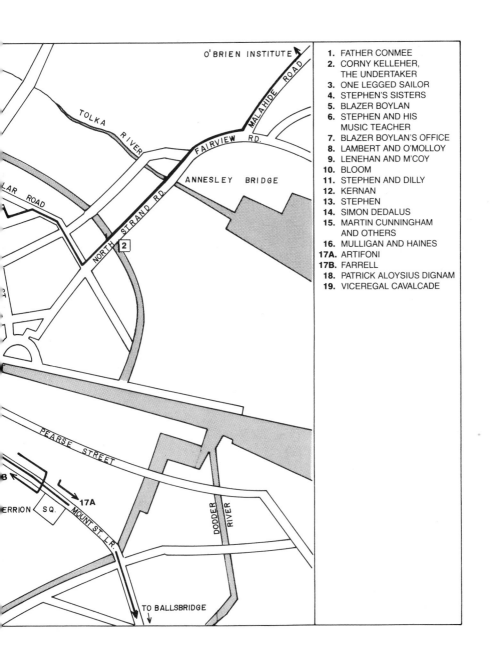

CHAPTER 10

O'BRIEN INSTITUTE

TOLKA RIVER

MALAHIDE ROAD

FAIRVIEW RD.

ANNESLEY BRIDGE

LAR ROAD

NORTH STRAND RD.

2

PEARSE STREET

B

17A

ERRION SQ.

MOUNT ST. LR.

DODDER RIVER

TO BALLSBRIDGE

1. FATHER CONMEE
2. CORNY KELLEHER,
   THE UNDERTAKER
3. ONE LEGGED SAILOR
4. STEPHEN'S SISTERS
5. BLAZER BOYLAN
6. STEPHEN AND HIS
   MUSIC TEACHER
7. BLAZER BOYLAN'S OFFICE
8. LAMBERT AND O'MOLLOY
9. LENEHAN AND M'COY
10. BLOOM
11. STEPHEN AND DILLY
12. KERNAN
13. STEPHEN
14. SIMON DEDALUS
15. MARTIN CUNNINGHAM
    AND OTHERS
16. MULLIGAN AND HAINES
17A. ARTIFONI
17B. FARRELL
18. PATRICK ALOYSIUS DIGNAM
19. VICEREGAL CAVALCADE

musichall' (232:37), officially the Empire Palace Theater, at No 72, and now called the Olympia Theater. They take another left just past the theater onto Sycamore Street, which runs into Essex Street East. Trying to find out what time it is, M'Coy looks into the 'sombre' office of Marcus Tertius Moses (233:14), a wholesale tea merchant at 30 Essex Street East, and then into the shop of another tea and wine merchant, J. J. O'Neill, on the opposite corner at 29 Essex Street East (both no longer there). Essex Street East becomes Temple Bar. They go under **Merchant's Arch**, a partially covered passageway from Temple Bar to Wellington Quay on the south side of the Liffey.

X: Here we see Bloom at a bookstall at **Merchant's Arch**, borrowing *Sweets of Sin* for Molly.

XI: Outside **Dillon's Auction Rooms** at No 25 Bachelor's Walk, Stephen's sister Dilly asks her father for some money and whether he has been in a nearby pub. Simon Dedalus criticizes her posture and says, 'I'll leave you all where Jesus left the jews' (238:32-33).

XII: As shown on the second map, this section charts the course of Tom Kernan from the sundial at the junction of James's Street and Bow Lane West to the Liffey via James's Street and Watling Street. A British sympathizer, Kernan works at Pulbrook, Robertson and Company, tea importers, 5 Leinster Chambers, No 43 Dame Street (which Joyce incorrectly lists as '5 Dame Street') and is seen walking towards his office. Having come from William C. Crimmins, tea, wine, and spirit merchant, 27 James's Street (now the Elm Lounge), he passes the offices of George Shackleton and Sons, flour millers and corn merchants, 35 **James's Street** (now no longer there); and Peter Kennedy, hairdresser at 48 James's Street (still occupied by a Kennedy, but this one is in the fish and poultry business). He sees from a distance the Church of St Catherine on Thomas Street where the Irish patriot Robert Emmet was executed by the British for his part in the abortive rising of 1803. Then he goes by the former site of the **Guinness Brewery** visitor's waiting room on the corner of James's and Watling Streets (a site now occupied by the Bank of Ireland) and the warehouses of the Dublin Distillers Co. at 21-32 Watling Street (which still owns the buildings, though the sign on the warehouse reads 'The Central Hide & Skin Co., Ltd.'). As Kernan approaches Island Street, he recalls how the Irish patriot Lord Edward Fitzgerald (1763-1798) hid from the British authorities in a nearby house (Nicholas Murphy's, 151-152 Thomas Street).

XIII: The narrative now turns to Stephen's journey down Fleet

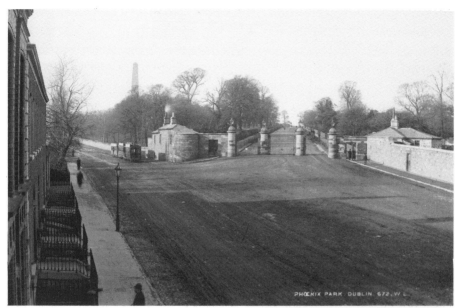

PHŒNIX PARK, DUBLIN. 672. W.L.

IN PHŒNIX PARK, DUBLIN. 2960. W.L.

Street, turning right onto Bedford Row. He is first seen looking in the window of Thomas Russell, a gem cutter at 57 Fleet Street (since demolished). He stops at **Clohissey's** bookstore at 10-11 Bedford Row to look at books and a print of a bare knuckle boxing match in 1860 that lasted thirty-seven rounds, and meets his sister Dilly.

XIV: In this episode Simon Dedalus talks with two acquaintances, Cowley and Dollard, outside **Reddy and Daughter's**, an antique shop at 19 Lower Ormond Quay, a two- or three-minute walk west from **Dillon's Auction Rooms**. Cowley is seeking Dollard's help in calling off two bailiffs sent by Reuben J. Dodd, the moneylender.

XV: Next we follow the short journey by Martin Cunningham and others from **Dublin Castle** to Kavanagh's Bar. The seat of British power in Ireland at the turn of the century, Dublin Castle was occupied by members of the Irish Citizen Army briefly during the 1916 Rising. Cunningham and his group walk northward about eighty yards from the castle entrance on Castle Street to find a carriage. Cunningham signals to the driver to pick them up nearby at the intersection of a street called Essex Gate. They walk east on Castle Street down Cork Hill past City Hall, which is still the seat of Dublin's city government. Going left at Parliament Street they walk past the offices of the *Dublin Evening Mail* (also occupied for a short time by Irish rebels in 1916), then an evening newspaper located at 38-40 Parliament Street and 'Mickey Anderson's watches' (246:39; Michael Anderson, Watchmaker at 30 Parliament Street), just before they reach Kavanagh's Bar at 27 Parliament Street (now a pub called Tommy Dunne's Tavern).

XVI: In this section, Stephen's two roommates at the Martello Tower, Mulligan and Haines, have cakes and scones at the **Dublin Bread Company's** tearoom at No 33 Dame Street (since demolished). Mulligan repeats a familiar joke, that the restaurant is called D.B.C. 'because they have damn bad cakes' (248:31).

They also see Charles Stewart Parnell's brother playing chess there; Joyce admired the way the dead leader used men like pawns.

XVII: Stephen's music teacher, Artifoni, is walking southeast along Mount Street Lower past Holles Street and **Sewell's Yard** – officially titled James Walter Sewell and Son and James Simpson, horse repository, commission, and livery establishment – at 60 Mount Street Lower. A well-known Dublin figure named Cashel Boyle O'Connor Fitzmaurice Tisdall Farrell follows (he was a constant character in Gogarty's *As I Was Going Down Sackville Street*). Farrell turns back at 'Mr Lewis Werner's cheerful windows' (250:5), a Georgian townhouse at 31 Merrion Square North on the corner of Holles Street (then the offices of Louis Werner, ophthalmic surgeon, now vacant); he stops in front of the former home of Oscar Wilde's parents, who lived at No 1 Merrion Square North (now the Dublin Document Exchange), and looks at the poster in front of Merrion Hall, on Merrion Street Lower, announcing the visit of an American evangelist. Farrell then strolls past 'Mr Bloom's dental windows' (250:14), the offices of Marcus J. Bloom, dental surgeon and lecturer on dental surgery, No 2 Clare Street (no relation to Leopold Bloom).

XVIII: Anxious to leave a house filled with funeral mourners, Paddy Dignam's son, Master Patrick Aloysius, goes on an errand to pick up a pound and a half of Mangan's pork steaks. Why he was sent almost two miles from their home is never explained, but in any case we see him walking home from **Mangan's Butcher Shop** at 1-2 William Street (the building has apparently survived but the ground floor now houses the Impressions Boutique) via Wicklow Street, Grafton Street, and Nassau Street. The butcher shop was located across the street from 'Ruggy O'Donohoe's' (250:20), actually M. O'Donohoe, International Bar, 23 Wicklow Street, on the corner of William Street (now just known as The International Bar). He looks in the 'window of Madame Doyle, court dress milliner' (250:29-30) at 33 Wicklow Street.

XIX: This last section is the 'curtain call' for the chapter. As the viceregal procession passes, almost every character in the 'Wandering Rocks' chapter 'salutes' the cavalcade. The viceroy goes from the Viceregal Lodge in Phoenix Park to attend the opening of the **Mirus Bazaar** in Ballsbridge, a journey of about five miles. As shown on the map, the carriages leave Phoenix Park at Park Gate, the south-eastern entrance of the park, and travel east along the quays that border the north side of the Liffey. The cavalcade goes over the Liffey at Grattan Bridge, along Parliament Street, then left onto Dame Street, past **Trinity**

College, eventually crossing the Grand Canal at Mount Street Bridge and entering Ballsbridge via Northumberland Road.

The first leg of the viceroy's journey passes several bridges that span the Liffey: Kings Bridge, named to commemorate King George IV's visit in 1821 and later officially renamed Sean Heuston Bridge in honour of an executed leader of the 1916 Rising; Bloody Bridge, the nickname for Victoria Bridge in Joyce's day, now named Rory O'More Bridge after a seventeenth-century Irish patriot; Queen's and Whitworth Bridges, the former named for George III's queen, Charlotte (now called Queen Maeve Bridge after a first-century Irish queen) and the latter honouring Earl Whitworth, a lord lieutenant of Ireland from 1813 to 1817 (now called Father Mathew Bridge after Rev. Theobald Mathew (1790-1856), a leader in the Irish temperance movement) and Richmond Bridge, located near the Four Courts at Winetavern Street and now named O'Donovan Rossa Bridge after Jeremiah O'Donovan Rossa (1831-1915), a Fenian leader whose funeral galvanized support for the 1916 Rising.

The viceroy and his party pass Dublin's legal center: the Four Courts, east of Whitworth Bridge; 'King's windows' (252:26) – William King, printer and law stationer, 36 Ormond Quay Upper; and Reuben J. Dodd, solicitor, at 34 Ormond Quay Upper (east of Richmond Bridge and still occupied on the upstairs level by solicitors). Also on Ormond Quay the procession passes the 'subsheriff's office' (252:32-33), the City of Dublin Sheriff's Office at No 30 (building demolished), and the **Ormond Hotel** at No 8. The cavalcade crosses the Liffey over Grattan Bridge, passing by Dollard's Printing House at 2-5 Wellington Quay (still called Dollard House, but now with lawyers and accountants for tenants) and 'Roger Greene's office' (252:39), a solicitor's office at No 11 Wellington Quay, still occupied by Roger Greene and Sons, Solicitors, located on the south bank of the Liffey and east of Grattan Bridge.

Going down Parliament Street, the entourage passes 'Lundy Foot's' (253:6; Lundy, Foot, and Co., wholesale tobacco and snuff manufacturers at No 26, at the intersection with Essex Gate, now the site of a bookmaker or 'turf accountant', G. C. Hackett),

59

Kavanagh's Bar at No 27, and Michael Anderson, Watchmaker at No 30, both of the latter mentioned in Section XV of this chapter. The cavalcade turns left onto Dame Street at Henry and James, clothiers at 1-3 Parliament Street and 82 Dame Street, and goes by the Marie Kendall poster at the Empire Palace (now Olympia) Theatre at No 72 Dame Street. At Fownes's Street, just before Dame Street becomes College Green, Stephen's sister Dilly sees them. Next passed on the route are 'King Billy's horse' (253:31), a statue of King William III (who defeated the Irish in the Battle of the Boyne in 1690) that once stood opposite **Trinity College** but has been replaced by a statue of Irish patriot Thomas Davis; 'Ponsonby's corner' (253:36-37) – Edward Ponsonby, seller of legal and general books, government agent and contractor, was at 116 Grafton Street (now a familiar stop for many American tourists since it houses the Dublin branch of American Express); and Pigott's music warerooms, 112 Grafton Street, site of Pigott and Company, pianoforte and musical instrument merchants, music sellers and publishers (the premises are now occupied by British Airways, but Pigott's still operates as McCullough Pigott at 11-13 Suffolk Street).

The carriages turn south onto Grafton Street and then immediately east (left) to Nassau Street, passing College Park in Trinity College and Finn's Hotel at 1-2 Leinster Street (Nassau Street becomes Leinster Street at the point). Joyce's wife, Nora, was working as a chambermaid at Finn's Hotel when they met on Nassau Street. Finn's Confectioners now occupies the premises, but a visitor can still see the name of Finn's Hotel on the Trinity College side of the building. At the back gate of Trinity College a porter touches his 'tallyho cap' (252:27) in deference to the viceroy – the porters of Trinity College today wear an odd-looking hat reminiscent of the East German police.

Past Trinity, Leinster Street becomes first Clare Street and then Merrion Square North, where the young Dignam boy raises his cap. The route concludes along Lower Mount Street and Northumberland Road past Haddington Road corner to the ultimate destination – the Royal Dublin Society (RDS) showgrounds, where the Mirus Bazaar was held.

Ormond Hotel
on the Liffey
3.38 P.M. TO 4.40 P.M.
(*Sirens*)

This 'musical' chapter (so called because it is packed with songs and musical references) takes place almost entirely at the **Ormond Hotel**, located at No 8 Ormond Quay Upper on the River Liffey. The hotel has been extensively remodeled since 1904. The chapter opens at the Ormond Bar with two barmaids talking. Bloom buys stationery at Daly's tobacconists at No 1 Ormond Quay Upper (to answer the letter from Martha Clifford), sees Boylan on Essex Bridge, now Grattan Bridge (better known as Capel Street Bridge) directly across the street from Daly's, and follows him to the Ormond Hotel. There he meets Richie Goulding (Stephen's uncle) in the bar and has something to eat. Boylan heads off for his meeting with Molly but Bloom stays and listens to the singing from the nearby barroom, where Simon Dedalus and some of his friends have gathered. Bloom then writes a short letter to Martha Clifford and leaves for an appointment at the **Green Street Courthouse**. The chapter ends with Bloom looking at a picture of Robert Emmet (the Irish patriot mentioned in Chapter Ten) in the window of Lionel Marks, an antique dealer a few doors away from the Ormond Hotel at No 16.

The map opposite shows Bloom's route from the **Merchant's Arch** bookstalls (which are still set up sporadically) to the Ormond Hotel and also his route from the hotel to the Green Street Courthouse. In the first of these journeys, Bloom is seen on the south bank of the Liffey, on Wellington Quay, walking west toward Grattan Bridge. Joyce describes this leg as follows: 'Bloowho went by by Moulang's pipes, bearing in his breast the sweets of sin, by Wine's antiques in memory bearing sweet sinful words, by Carroll's dusky battered plate, for Raoul.' (258:9-

11). The shops mentioned here are Bernard Wine, general dealer in jewelry and antiquities, No 35 Wellington Quay (now part of Wellington Office Supply Ltd.); Daniel Moulang, jeweler and pipe importer, at No 31 (now occupied by opticians Henry Maude and Mrs B. Culliton); and John Carroll, watchmaker, jeweler, and dealer in old plate, at No 29 (now another optician, Errol Victor Little). Next, 'Bloowhose dark eye read Aaron Figatner's name. Why do I always think Figather? Gathering figs I think. And Prosper Loré's huguenot name. By Bassi's blessed virgins Bloom's dark eyes went by.' (259:37-40): Aaron Figatner was a diamond setter and jeweler at 26 Wellington Quay (now the Northlight Razor Blade Co.); Prosper Loré, a wholesale hat manufacturer at No 22; and Aurelio Bassi a statue and picture-frame maker at No 14 (the site still occupied by A. Bassi & Co., Ltd., religious goods). The last establishments along Wellington Quay that Joyce mentions are Cantwell and M'Donald, wholesale wine and whiskey merchants and rectifying distillers, at No 12 (now Cyril O'Neill, legal cost accountants); and the Clarence Commercial Hotel at Nos 6-7 (still operating as the Clarence Hotel and now expanded to occupy No 8 as well). Here Bloom crosses over Grattan Bridge and stops at Daly's, now a Bank of Ireland office. He sees Blazes Boylan on the bridge, riding in a 'jauntingcar' (263:41) that stops at the Ormond Hotel; he follows Boylan there.

In the second journey, Bloom leaves the Ormond at about 4.30 p.m. He turns right, walking up the quay past J. M. Barry and Co., merchant tailors and outfitters (12 Ormond Quay Upper) and Lionel Marks, antique dealer – both gone now – and mails his letter to Martha Clifford at the post office. He turns right on Chancery Street, then onto Greek Street to Mary's Lane and left into Green Street. The map also depicts Blazes Boylan's route from the hotel to Bloom's house (**No 7 Eccles Street**) for his rendezvous with Molly.

How to get there: see locations on index map. Merchant's Arch is a ten minute walk from O'Connell Street.

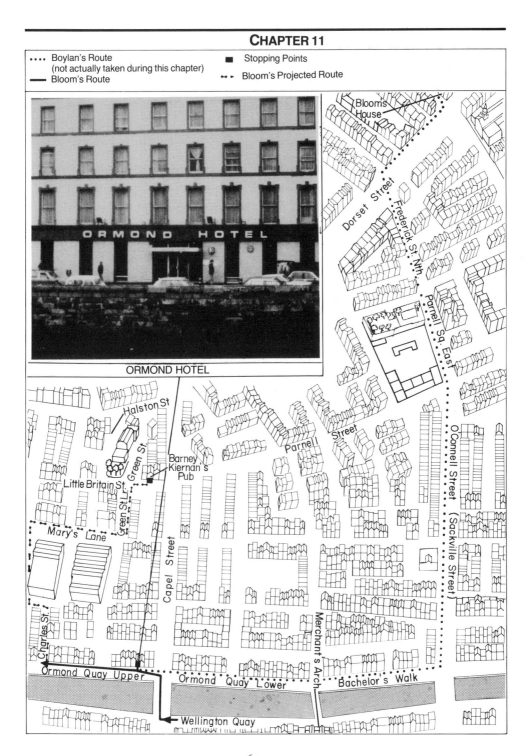

CHAPTER 11

Boylan's Route
(not actually taken during this chapter)
— Bloom's Route
■ Stopping Points
►•► Bloom's Projected Route

ORMOND HOTEL

Blooms House

Dorset Street

Frederick St. Nth

Parnell Sq. East

O'Connell Street (Sackville Street)

Halston St

Green St.

Barney Kiernan's Pub

Little Britain St.

Green St Lr.

Mary's Lane

Parnell Street

Capel Street

Charles St.

Merchant's Arch

Ormond Quay Upper

Ormond Quay Lower

Bachelor's Walk

Wellington Quay

Barney Kiernan's Pub
4.45 P.M. TO 5.45 P.M.
(Cyclops)

This chapter (which is narrated by an unnamed Dublin debt collector) is set in **Barney Kiernan's Pub**, formerly located at 8-10 Little Britain Street (near the corner of Green Street). Bloom arrives at the pub expecting to meet two others whom he will accompany to the widowed Mrs Dignam's house near Sandymount Strand. At the bar is 'the citizen', who is based on a Dublin character named Michael Cusack (1847-1907), the founder of the Gaelic Athletic Association, set up to promote Gaelic sports such as hurling and Gaelic football. He is accompanied by his dog, Garryowen, of whom the narrator remarks that it would be a 'corporal work of mercy if someone would take the life of that bloody dog' (295:18-19). Bloom has a quarrel with the citizen concerning the Jewish religion, Irish politics, and whether or not Bloom should buy a round of drinks. Enraged, the citizen chases Bloom and throws a biscuit tin at him, in a broad parody of the Cyclops episode in Homer's *Odyssey*.

The illustration on the facing page details the route taken by the narrator from the 'corner of Arbour Hill' (292:2. at the intersection with a street called Stoney Batter, where the chapter starts to Barney Kiernan's pub, now much reduced and currently a unisex hairdresser called 'As You Like It'. The narrator and a companion named Joe Hynes walk east from Arbour Hill along King Street North (going a short distance on Stoney Batter) and then turn south (right) on Halston Street to Little Britain Street. They pass the Linenhall Barracks – a series of buildings that were formerly bounded by King Street North – Coleraine Street, Lisburn Street, and 'the back of the courthouse' (293:33-34) – the **Civil Bill** or **Recorder's Court** on Halston Street, which fronted on 26 Green Street, now occupied by the Special Criminal Court.

How to get there: see index map. Or take bus nos. 37/39 from Middle Abbey Street.

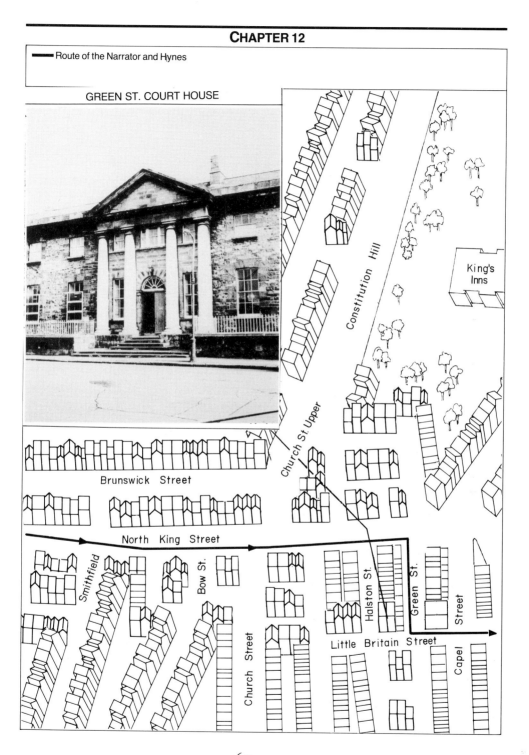

CHAPTER 12

Route of the Narrator and Hynes

GREEN ST. COURT HOUSE

Constitution Hill

King's Inns

Church St. Upper

Brunswick Street

North King Street

Smithfield

Bow St.

Church Street

Halston St.

Green St.

Little Britain Street

Capel Street

SANDYMOUNT STRAND AGAIN
8.00 P.M. TO 9.00 P.M.
(Nausicaa)

After arriving at Paddy Dignam's house at **No. 9 Newbridge Avenue** in Sandymount shortly before 6.00 p.m., Bloom spends approximately two hours with Mrs Dignam and agrees to help the family in settling the estate. He then walks down to **Sandymount Strand**, the same beach along which Stephen walked in Chapter Three. Partly written in a style parodying popular romantic magazines of Joyce's time, this chapter starts with a scene describing three girls taking some children out to play on the beach. When Bloom arrives, one of the girls, Gerty MacDowell, realizes that he is watching her; she leans back to watch a fireworks display and purposely lets Bloom see under her dress. Bloom becomes sexually aroused and at this point the style of the chapter changes. We now follow Bloom's stream of consciousness as he speculates about everything from girls' secret thoughts to life in the ocean ('Do fish ever get seasick?' 379:1-2) until the chapter ends with Bloom falling asleep, as nine cuckoos are heard from a nearby cuckoo clock.

The map on the opposite page shows the path that Bloom took from Dignam's house to Sandymount Strand via Leahy's Terrace. In 1904 Bloom had only to cross over from Leahy's Terrace to reach the Strand. Since then much of it has been reclaimed from the sea. The visitor today must turn right and walk some distance along Beach Road before reaching the sea.

How to get there: by DART train from Amiens Street station; Tara Street station; Westland Row station to Lansdowne Road station. Or take the No. 3 bus from O'Connell Street.

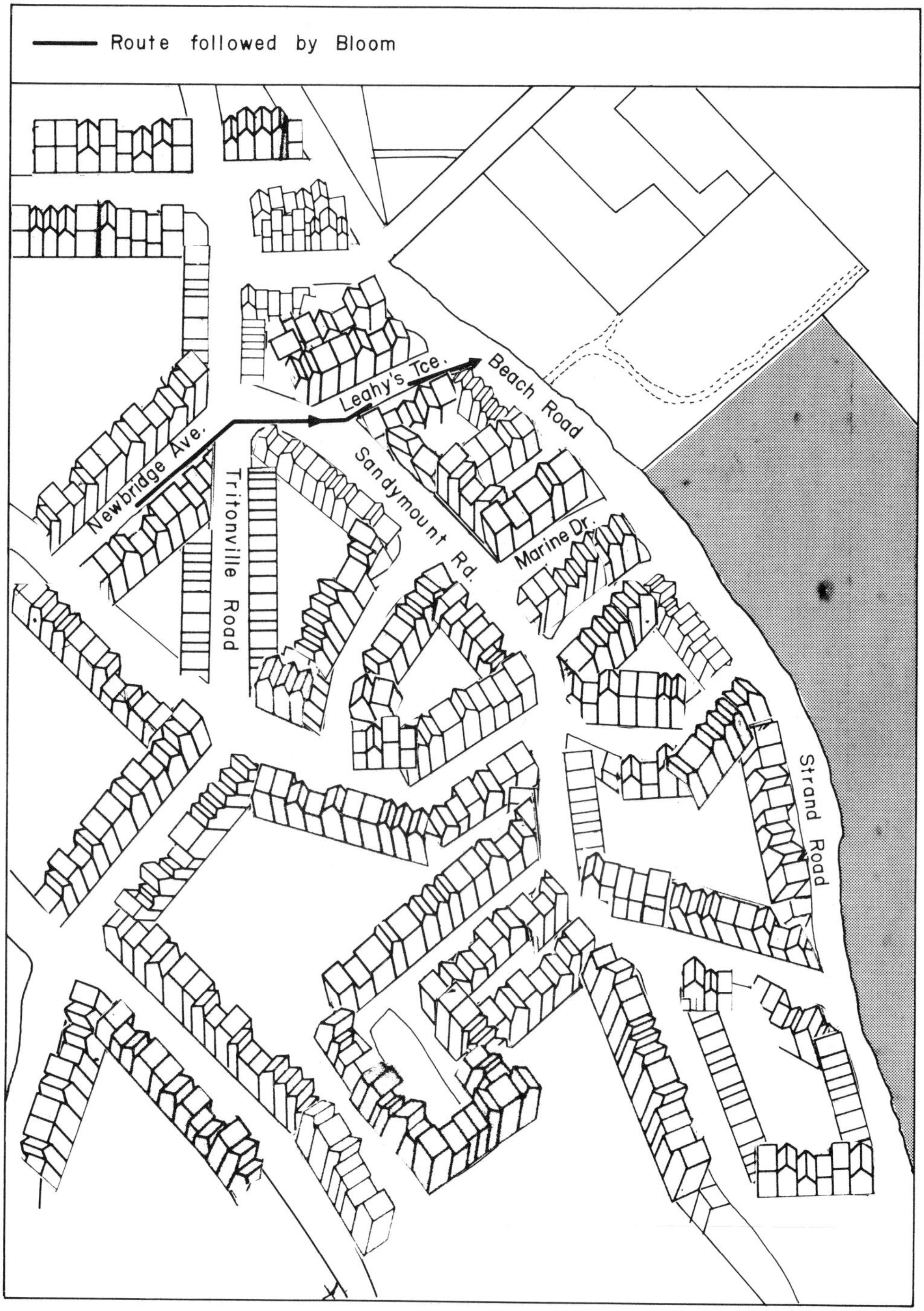

CHAPTER 13

——— Route followed by Bloom

Newbridge Ave.

Leahy's Tce.

Beach Road

Tritonville Road

Sandymount Rd.

Marine Dr.

Strand Road

HOLLES STREET

10.00 P.M. TO 11.00 P.M.

(Oxen of the Sun)

This chapter traces both the nine months of pregnancy and the various stages in the development of the English language. Bloom returns to the center of Dublin via the Sandymount (Haddington Road) tram, which would drop him very close to the main entrance of the **National Maternity Hospital** in Holles Street. This hospital is still in existence (though totally rebuilt in the classical style after Joyce's departure) and is where most of the chapter takes place. After some incantations to the god of fertility, the chapter opens with Bloom asking at the hospital about his friend, Mrs Purefoy, who has been in labor there for three days. Once again Bloom encounters Stephen Dedalus, who is at the hospital drinking with some medical students. Bloom decides to keep an eye on him. When the baby is born just before 11.00 p.m., Stephen and his companions leave the hospital, cross Holles Street, and walk north to have drinks at **Burke's Pub** on the corner of Holles Street and Denzille Lane. After closing time at Burke's, Stephen and a friend named Lynch head toward the **Westland Row station** (Pearse station), where they will take a train to **Amiens Street station** (Connolly station), the stop closest to what was in 1904 the brothel area of Dublin (but is now mostly public housing projects). Bloom follows Stephen from the hospital to the pub and then to the train station.

The map opposite shows the location of the National Maternity Hospital on Holles Street and the spot where Burke's Pub stood at 17 Holles Street. It also details the route that Stephen (followed by Bloom) takes to get from Burke's Pub to the Westland Row station via Holles Street, Denzille Lane, Fenian Street, and Westland Row.

How to get there: see on index map. Take Nos. 7/8 bus from Eden Quay.

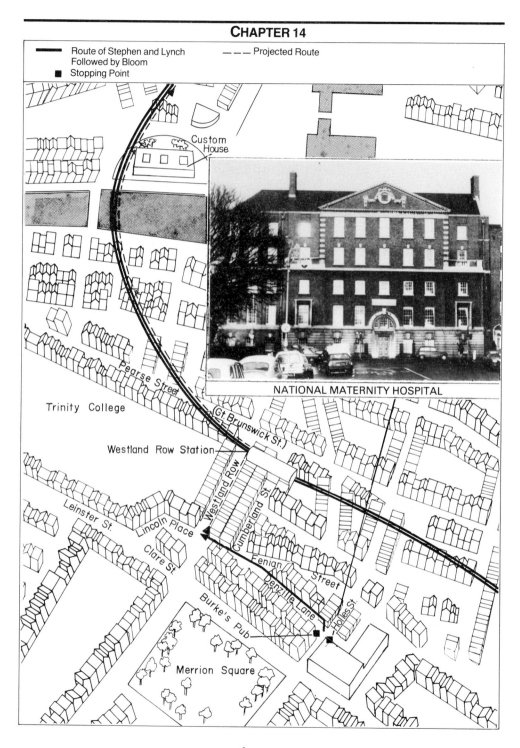

CHAPTER 14

Route of Stephen and Lynch
Followed by Bloom
■ Stopping Point
— — — Projected Route

Custom House

NATIONAL MATERNITY HOSPITAL

Pearse Street

Trinity College

(Gt Brunswick St.)

Westland Row Station

Westland Row

Cumberland St.

Leinster St.

Lincoln Place

Clare St.

Fenian Street

Denzille Lane

Holes St.

Burke's Pub

Merrion Square

Nighttown

12.00 MIDNIGHT TO 1.00 A.M.

(Circe)

At about a quarter past eleven, Stephen and Lynch reach the Westland Row (Pearse) station and travel by train to the **Amiens Street** (Connolly) **station**. They walk to **Bella Cohen's** via Talbot Street and Mabbot Street (now known as Corporation Street) or, in the opening words of the chapter, 'The Mabbot Street entrance of nighttown' (429:1). Joyce apparently coined the term 'night-town' to refer to this brothel area of Dublin. Most Dubliners referred to the area as 'Monto' after Montgomery Street, which ran through the district. This once-famous area of Dublin was eliminated in the 1920s, and a visitor there today would see

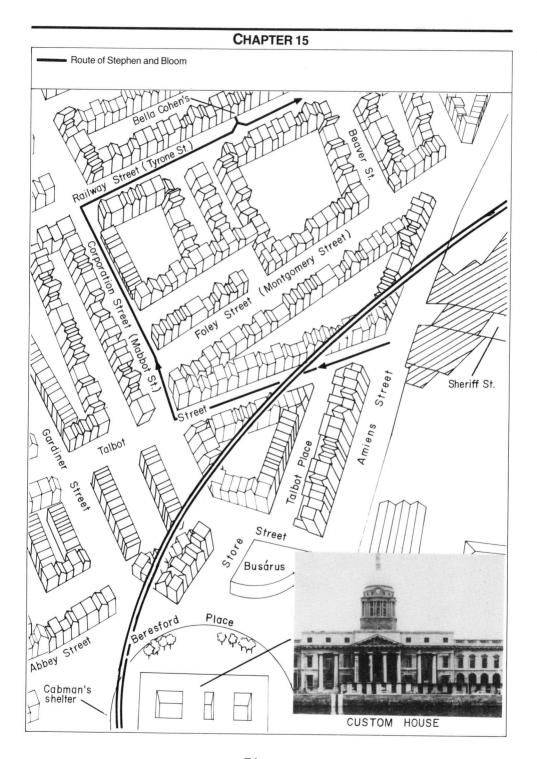

CHAPTER 15

Route of Stephen and Bloom

Bella Cohen's

Railway Street (Tyrone St.)

Beaver St.

Corporation Street (Mabbot St.)

Foley Street (Montgomery Street)

Sheriff St.

Street

Amiens Street

Talbot Place

Gardiner Street

Talbot

Store Street

Busárus

Beresford Place

Abbey Street

Cabman's shelter

CUSTOM HOUSE

71

public housing projects. Bloom misses the stop at Amiens Street station and must get off at the next stop. By the time he returns to Amiens Street (presumably by the next incoming train) he has to hurry to catch up with Stephen and Lynch. He finally tracks them down at Bella Cohen's at 82 Tyrone Street Lower (now called Railway Street), where Stephen is playing the piano, drinking, and dancing. After Stephen leaves Bella Cohen's, he gets into an altercation with a British soldier. The soldier knocks him down and Bloom comes to Stephen's assistance. The chapter ends with Bloom standing paternal guard over Stephen, who has collapsed from drink and exhaustion.

The map on page 71 shows the path that both Stephen and Bloom take from the **Amiens Street station** via Talbot Street, Mabbot Street and then Tyrone Street Lower. The map also pinpoints the location of **Bella Cohen's**; but as with most of the structures and trades of nighttown it no longer exists.

How to get there: see location on index map. Within walking distance of O'Connell Street.

CABMAN'S SHELTER

1.00 A.M. TO 2.00 A.M.

(*Eumaeus*)

Written in a rambling, wordy style evocative of the character's weariness and the lateness of the hour, this chapter opens with Bloom finally meeting Stephen and helping him off the pavement near Bella Cohen's house at 82 Tyrone Street Lower. Bloom and Stephen then go to a coffee stall near the Liffey. There Bloom buys Stephen a coffee and bun, and they listen to an old sailor telling stories. Bloom offers to put Stephen up for the night. Both are tired when they begin their walk to his house (about a mile away) as the chapter ends.

The map on page 75 shows their way from Tyrone Street Lower (now Railway Street) to the **cabman's shelter**, a dingy wooden structure that was located at Butt Bridge serving rudimentary refreshments principally to cab drivers. Joyce describes their walk 'together along Beaver street . . . as far as the farrier's and the distinctly fetid atmosphere of the livery stables at the corner of Montgomery street where they made tracks to the left from thence debouching into Amiens street round by the corner of Dan Bergin's' (613:25-29). The farrier's was J. Kavanagh, horse-shoer, at 14-15 Beaver Street; and Daniel L. Bergin, grocer, tea and wine merchant, was at No. 46 Amiens Street on the corner of Montgomery Street (Foley Street), now a pub occupied by L. Lloyd. Bloom sees a horse-drawn cab outside the North Star Hotel, still located at 26-30 Amiens Street across from the railway station; but, unable to get the cabbie's attention, decides to walk instead, passing the premises of John Mullet, tea, wine, and spirit merchant at 45 Amiens Street (today it still bears that name) and the Signal House (the establishment of Thomas F. Hayden, family grocer and spirit merchant, 36 Amiens Street, now J. and M. Cleary, vintners). They go by the Amiens Street station (Connolly station), the back door of the morgue (the

Dublin City Morgue at 2-4 Amiens Street, still there), and the Dock Tavern (run by Mrs M. A. Hall at No. 1 Store Street on the corner of Amiens Street, now the Master Mariner Bar). They turn right (west) on Store Street past the C Division police station (the Dublin Metropolitan Police Barrack, 3 Store Street, on the corner of Mabbot Street, now Corporation Street) and the City Bakery run by James Rourke at 5-6 Store Street (now the head office of Kylemore Bakery Ltd.). After Store Street they come to Beresford Place, which curves around the back of the **Custom House** to end at Butt Bridge near the **cabman's shelter**.

The map also depicts the route Bloom and Stephen follow when they start off towards Bloom's house, from the cabman's shelter, around Beresford Place, to Gardiner Street Lower. Although the cabman's shelter, described as an 'unpretentious wooden structure' (621:34), no longer exists, the Amiens Street station and the Custom House still look much the same as they did in 1904.

How to get there: see location on index map. Within walking distance of O'Connell Street.

CHAPTER 16

Route of Stephen and Bloom

Bella Cohen's

Railway Street (Tyrone St.)

Beaver St.

Corporation Street (Mabbot St.)

Foley Street (Montgomery Street)

Sheriff St.

Amiens Street

Talbot Place

Talbot Street

Gardiner Street

Store Street

Busárus

Beresford Place

Abbey Street

Cabman's shelter

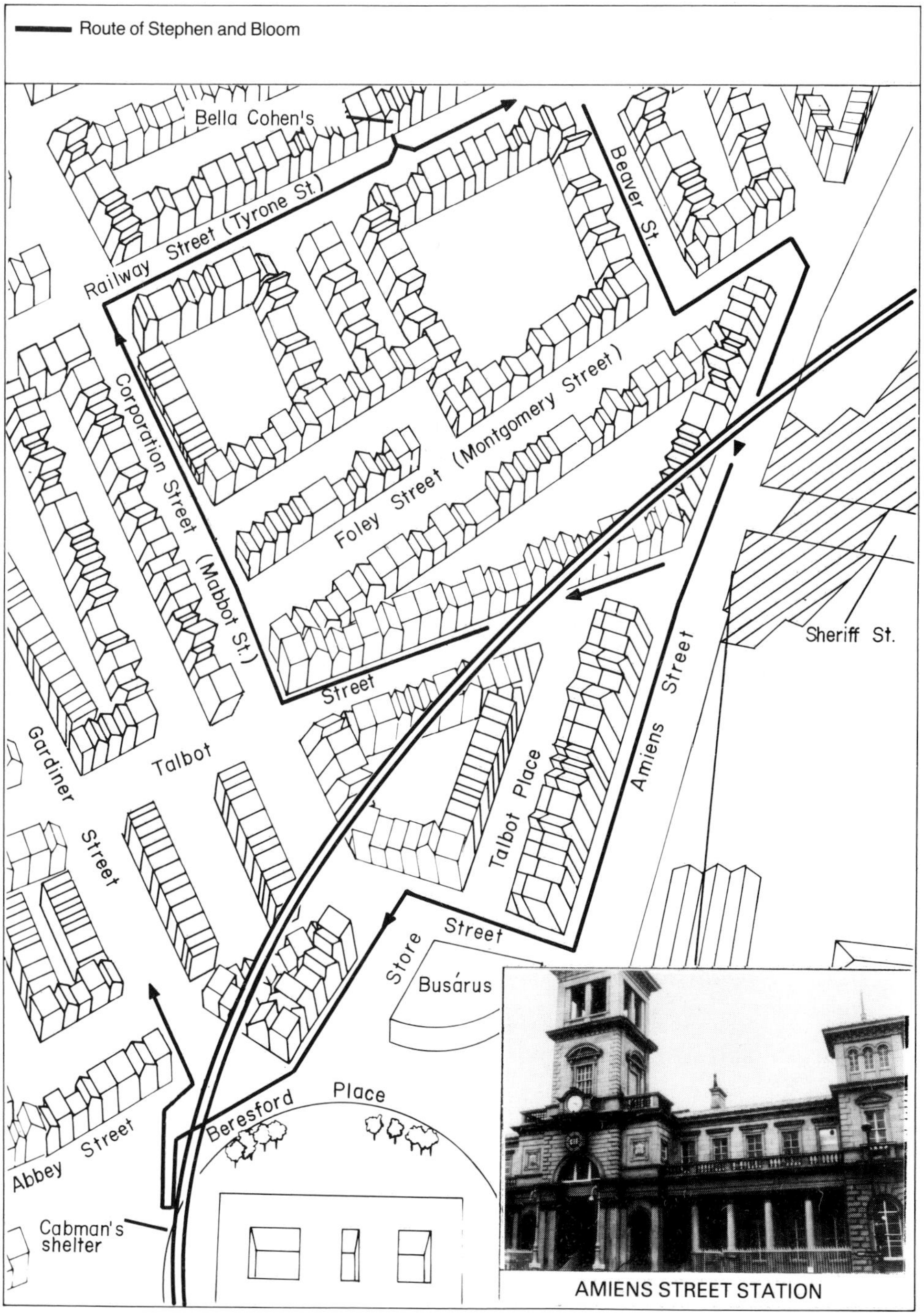

AMIENS STREET STATION

75

HOME

2.00 A.M. TO 2.45 A.M.

(Ithaca)

This chapter, which opens with Bloom and Stephen walking to Bloom's house at **No 7 Eccles Street**, is written in a question-and-answer style reminiscent of a catechism. Arriving at his house, Bloom finds he has forgotten to take a house key and must climb over a railing and lower himself to a basement-level door to get into his house. Bloom takes Stephen down to the kitchen and gives him cocoa. They talk. Stephen refuses the offer of a place to stay for the night and departs. Bloom gets ready for bed, then lying alongside but in the opposite direction to his wife Molly he tells her about some of the day's events before falling asleep.

The map opposite, shows Stephen and Bloom's route from the **cabman's shelter**. Joyce describes it in the first question and answer in the episode: Bloom and Stephen walk north and east along Beresford Place, then north along Lower Gardiner Street and its extensions, Middle Gardiner Street and Mountjoy Square West. They turn left (west) on Gardiner Place and then right into Temple Street North, which curves around the front of St. George's Church and runs into Eccles Street, where Bloom lives at No 7.

How to get there: see location on index map. Within walking distance of O'Connell Street.

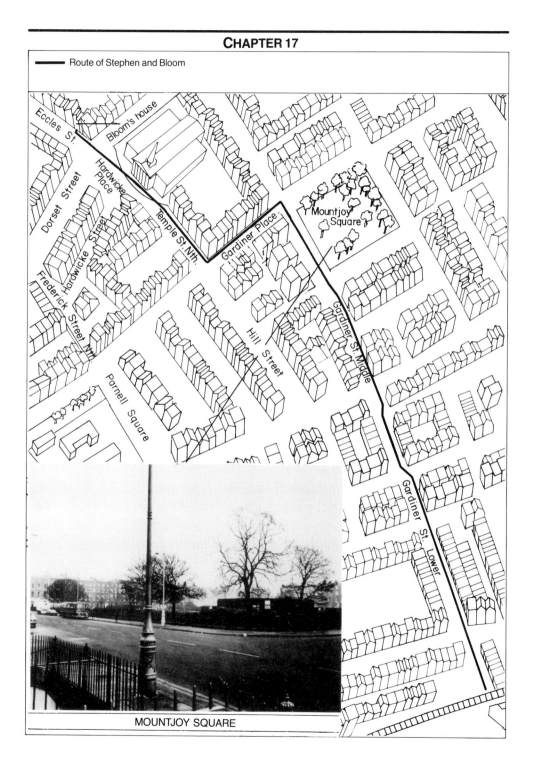

CHAPTER 17

Route of Stephen and Bloom

Eccles St.

Bloom's house

Hardwicke Place

Dorset Street

Temple St. Nth.

Hardwicke Street

Gardiner Place

Mountjoy Square

Frederick Hardwicke

Frederick Street Nth.

Hill Street

Gardiner St. Middle

Parnell Square

Gardiner St. Lower

MOUNTJOY SQUARE

MOLLY'S BEDROOM
ABOUT 2.00 A.M. TO 2.17 A.M.
(Penelope)

The final chapter consists of a soliloquy by Molly Bloom. While her husband sleeps, Molly lies awake thinking. From her bed Molly completes her own odyssey: an odyssey of the mind. As she journeys back over the events of the day to more distant memories she refers to over 50 locations in Dublin city and its environs and remembers also some of the more exotic places in Gibraltar where she lived as a girl.

The map shows some of the places in Dublin she mentions in passing. **Westland Row chapel**: where Molly remembers seeing the young medical student who had shown an interest in her when she and Bloom lived in Holles Street. (The subject of love and seduction is never far from Molly's thoughts for 'a woman wants to be embraced 20 times a day almost to make her look young no matter by who so long as to be in love or loved by somebody . . .') **Switzers**: still a thriving department store in Grafton Street; it was quite likely one of Molly's favourite places, as she admits 'I love the smell of a rich big shop'.

As Molly recalls her first introduction to Blazes Boylan in the D.B.C. tea shop in Dame Street, she is reminded also that that was the day on which she lost her best pair of suede gloves and scoffs once more at the suggestion Bloom had made then: that she advertise for their return in *The Irish Times*, then located in Westmoreland Street, now in D'Olier Street.

Molly, toying with the idea of a younger lover, Stephen Dedalus perhaps? remembers seeing him as a child with his parents at **Kingsbridge** station (now Heuston Station).

CHAPTER 18

1. IRISH TIMES BUILDING, D'OLIER ST.   4. KINGSBRIDGE STATION
2. WESTLAND ROW CHAPEL
3. SWITZER'S WINDOW, GRAFTON ST.

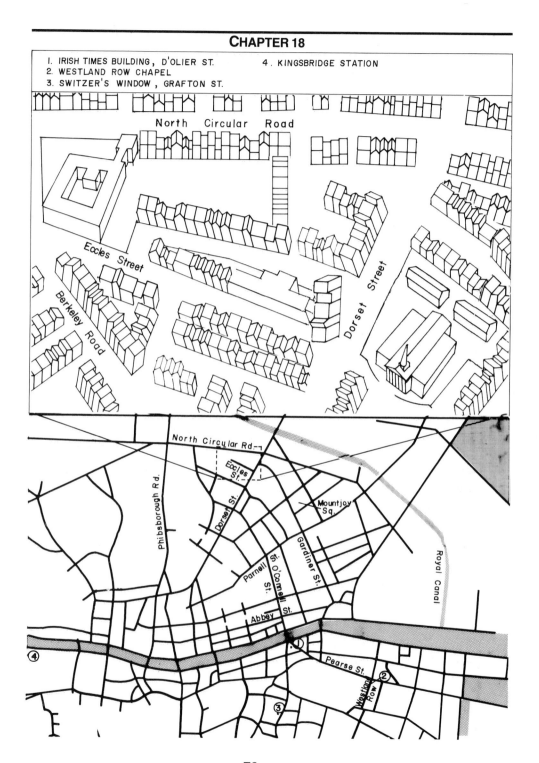

INDEX

An index to some Joycean places still to be seen in Dublin (as of 1986), and referred to in this book.